DRAMA CLA

The Drama Classics .... atest
plays in affordable p............................. students, actors
and theatregoers. The hallmarks of the series are accessible
introductions, uncluttered texts and an overall theatrical
perspective.

Given that readers may be encountering a particular play
for the first time, the introduction seeks to fill in the
theatrical/historical background and to outline the chief
themes rather than concentrate on interpretational and
textual analysis. Similarly the play-texts themselves are free
of footnotes and other interpolations: instead there is an
end-glossary of 'difficult' words and phrases.

The texts of the English-language plays in the series
have been prepared taking full account of all existing
scholarship. The foreign-language plays have been newly
translated into a modern English that is both actable and
accurate: many of the translators regularly have their work
staged professionally.

Edited until his early death by Kenneth McLeish, the
Drama Classics series continues with his aim of providing a
first-class library of dramatic literature representing the best
of world theatre.

Associate editors:
Professor Trevor R. Griffiths
Visiting Professor in Humanities, University of Hertfordshire
Dr Colin Counsell
School of Humanities, Arts and Languages,
London Metropolitan University

DRAMA CLASSICS *the first hundred*

The Alchemist
All for Love
Andromache
Antigone
Arden of Faversham
Bacchae
Bartholomew Fair
The Beaux Stratagem
The Beggar's Opera
Birds
Celestina
The Changeling
A Chaste Maid in
    Cheapside
The Cherry Orchard
Children of the Sun
El Cid
The Country Wife
The Dance of Death
The Devil is an Ass
Doctor Faustus
A Doll's House
Don Juan
The Duchess of
    Malfi
Edward II
Electra (Euripides)
Electra (Sophocles)
An Enemy of the
    People
Every Man in his
    Humour
Everyman
Faust
A Flea in her Ear
Frogs
Fuenteovejuna
The Game of Love
    and Chance
Ghosts
The Government
    Inspector

Hecuba
Hedda Gabler
The Hypochondriac
The Importance of
    Being Earnest
An Ideal Husband
An Italian Straw Hat
The Jew of Malta
The Knight of the
    Burning Pestle
The Lady from the Sea
The Learned Ladies
Lady Windermere's
    Fan
Life is a Dream
The Lower Depths
The Lucky Chance
Lulu
Lysistrata
The Magistrate
The Malcontent
The Man of Mode
The Marriage of
    Figaro
Mary Stuart
The Master Builder
Medea
The Misanthrope
The Miser
Miss Julie
A Month in the
    Country
A New Way to Pay
    Old Debts
Oedipus
The Oresteia
Peer Gynt
Phedra
The Playboy of the
    Western World
The Recruiting
    Officer

The Revenger's
    Tragedy
The Rivals
The Roaring Girl
La Ronde
Rosmersholm
The Rover
Scapino
The School for
    Scandal
The Seagull
The Servant of Two
    Masters
She Stoops to Conquer
The Shoemakers'
    Holiday
Six Characters in Search
    of an Author
The Spanish Tragedy
Spring's Awakening
Summerfolk
Tartuffe
Three Sisters
'Tis Pity She's a
    Whore
Too Clever by Half
Ubu
Uncle Vanya
Volpone
The Way of the
    World
The White Devil
The Wild Duck
A Woman of No
    Importance
Women Beware
    Women
Women of Troy
Woyzeck

*The publishers welcome
suggestions for further titles*

DRAMA CLASSICS

LA RONDE

by

Arthur Schnitzler

translated and introduced by
Stephen Unwin and Peter Zombory-Moldovan

NICK HERN BOOKS

London

www.nickhernbooks.co.uk

A Drama Classic

This edition of *La Ronde* first published in Great Britain in 2007 as a paperback original by Nick Hern Books, 14 Larden Road, London W3 7ST

Typeset by Country Setting, Kingsdown, Kent CT14 8ES
Printed in Great Britain by CPI Bookmarque, Croydon, Surrey

A CIP catalogue record for this book is available from the British Library

ISBN 978 1 85459 587 4

Introduction

Arthur Schnitzler (1862-1931)

Arthur Schnitzler was born in Vienna on 15 May 1862, the eldest child of Louise and Professor Johann Schnitzler, a distinguished laryngologist. His maternal grandfather, Philip Markbreiter, had also been a doctor, and Arthur was expected to follow in their footsteps. He studied medicine at the University of Vienna and served as an army medical officer for a year. He took up a junior clinical post at the Vienna General Hospital and edited a medical journal founded by his father.

His interest in medicine was limited from the outset, and after his father's death in 1893 he confined himself to private practice. He was, however, drawn to the emerging science of psychiatry and wrote a paper on speech loss and its treatment by hypnosis. His interest in Sigmund Freud's exploration of the unconscious mind also informs much of his literary work.

With anti-Semitism on the rise in Vienna from the 1880s, Schnitzler – who dismissed all religion as dogma – was never allowed to forget his Jewish ancestry. His circle of friends included many of the great literary figures of the day. He corresponded with Rainer Maria Rilke, Georg Brandes and Hugo von Hofmannstahl, among many others. He visited London, Paris and Berlin, and called on Henrik Ibsen in Norway in 1896.

His private life was complex. He had relationships with numerous women – often at the same time – including a stormy affair with the actress Adele Sandrock. He fell in love with one of his patients, Marie Reinhard, who gave birth to their stillborn child in 1897. In 1899 he met and married the actress Olga Gussmann, with whom he had a son, Heinrich, and a daughter, Lili; they divorced in 1921. Throughout his life he kept a diary (the manuscript runs to some 8,000 pages) remarkable for its frank descriptions of his many sexual encounters; it includes, for a while, a record of every orgasm.

Schnitzler's first major dramatic work, *Anatol*, a cycle of one-act plays, was completed in 1892. This was soon followed by *Liebelei* (sometimes translated as 'Flirtations') in 1894 and *Reigen* (*La Ronde*) in 1897; these, along with his study of anti-Semitism, *Professor Bernhardi* (1912), are the plays for which he is best known. Others include *The Green Cockatoo* (1899), *The Lonely Way* (1904) and his last stage play, *The Walk to the Fish Pond* (1931). He also wrote prose works, including two collections of stories, *The Greek Dancing Girl* (1905) and *Souls in Twilight* (1907), as well as a number of novellas; the best known are *Dying* (1894), *Fräulein Else* (1924), *Dream Story* (1926), and *Therese: A Chronicle of a Woman's Life* (1928). His *Book of Maxims and Doubts, Aphorisms and Fragments* appeared in 1927; his memoir, *My Youth in Vienna*, was published in 1968.

Many of his plays were premiered at Vienna's prestigious Burgtheater and were, for the most part, critically and commercially successful. He was, however, no stranger to controversy: he was forced to give up his army commission following the publication in 1901 of his satirical novel *Lieutenant Gustl* (which was said to have 'tarnished the image of the Austro-Hungarian army'), and *La Ronde* was the subject of widely publicised criminal proceedings in Berlin in 1921 (see below, 'The Struggle for Acceptance').

Schnitzler's last years were overshadowed by the suicide in 1928 of his daughter, Lili. His last novel, *Flight into Darkness*, was published in 1931. He died of a brain haemorrhage the same year in Vienna on 21 October.

Vienna 1900

The Austro-Hungarian Empire of 1867-1918 stretched from the Alps to the Russian steppe and from the forests of Poland to the shores of the Adriatic. Schnitzler's Vienna was its political, economic and cultural capital. The city was home to the glittering Hapsburg court and a large and prosperous middle class. It had grown rapidly following the revolutions of 1848, with migrants drawn from every corner of the Empire by the city's cosmopolitan energy, its reputation for tolerance and the opportunities for material and social advancement it could offer. Of a population in 1910 of over two million, one in ten was Jewish by faith or descent; although the recent influx of mainly Galician Jews had little in common with the assimilated and much wealthier minority prominent in the city's academic, professional and cultural life.

Construction of the majestic Ringstrasse (Ring Boulevard) had started in 1857, and the city boasted magnificent new imperial and civic buildings, a thriving university, and a world-famous opera house and theatre. Vienna prided itself on catering for the civilised pleasures of urban life: its spacious parks and popular entertainments were thronged at weekends, middle-class audiences flocked to the latest operettas and the aristocratic splendour of the New Year Ball was legendary. The city's elegant restaurants and, above all, its coffee-houses played a central part in its vibrant social, cultural and intellectual life.

Cautious political reforms following Austria's defeat in the Austro-Prussian War of 1866 had given Vienna a degree of political stability. The stock exchange crash of 1873, however, led to a twenty-year depression and, by the 1880s, the deficiencies of the all-powerful but sclerotic imperial system were starting to show. Society was rocked by a series of royal and political scandals. The narrow electoral franchise, which restricted voting rights to the educated and well-off, was coming under concerted attack, together with the Liberal political ascendancy which it had produced. In 1895 the populist demagogue Karl Lueger (1844-1910) was elected mayor of Vienna, and in 1901 twenty-one members of Georg von Schönerer's (1842-1921) virulently anti-Semitic Pan-German Party entered Parliament.

This combination of bourgeois complacency with increasing political instability was the setting for an extraordinary artistic, scientific and philosophical flowering, a 'golden age' in which, according to Stefan Zweig's memoirs, 'the desire for culture was more passionate than in other European cities'. Its chief characteristic (perhaps in reaction to the increasing tensions in the body politic) was a tendency to look inward rather than outward, most notably illustrated by the pioneering exploration of the subconscious undertaken by Josef Breuer (1842-1925) and, pre-eminently, Sigmund Freud (1856-1939), in whose home the *Mittwochsgesellschaft* ('Wednesday Society'), the precursor of the Vienna Psychoanalytical Society, held its weekly meetings from 1901.

Vienna had long been a centre, also, of musical excellence. As the old century was drawing to a close, the waltzes of Johann Strauss II (1825-99), with their hint of sweet melancholy, captured the city's hedonistic self-image and its fondness for sentimentality; the operetta was the great popular form, with Franz Lehár's (1870-1948) masterpiece *The Merry Widow* premiered at the Theater an der Wien in 1905; while the more challenging symphonies of Gustav Mahler (1860-1911) and the early, difficult, music of Arnold Schoenberg (1874-1951) tested the limits of popular taste.

Meanwhile, the conservatism evident in the visual arts was challenged by the *Secession*, a society founded in 1897 by nineteen young artists and architects in reaction to (or secession from) the prevailing Academic tradition, which favoured historical subjects and styles. Its first president was Gustav Klimt (1862-1914); other key members were the architects and designers Josef Hoffmann (1870-1956), Otto Wagner (1841-1918) and Josef Maria Olbrich (1867-1908). The movement embraced the *Jugendstil*, a distinctive variant of the *Art Nouveau* style current in Paris. In 1903 Klimt and a number of others broke off from the *Secession* and set up the *Wiener Werkstätte* (Vienna Workshops), with the aim of reforming product design: among its leading figures was the painter Egon Schiele (1890-1918). One of the most significant architects of the period, Adolf Loos (1870-1933), whose provocative manifesto was entitled *Ornament and Crime*, belonged to neither group.

By the standards of Britain, France and Russia, nineteenth-century Austrian literature was relatively undistinguished. In 1890, however, a group of young writers – including Schnitzler, Peter Altenberg (1859-1919) and Hugo von Hofmannsthal (1874-1929) – formed *Jung-Wien* (Young Vienna), a progressive literary society which met in the famous Café Griensteidl. The group later included the young Stefan Zweig (1881-1942) and, until he turned against it, Karl Kraus (1874-1936), the influential editor and financier of the provocative satirical magazine *Die Fackel (The Torch)*.

Turn-of-the-century Vienna saw extraordinary levels of artistic innovation and achievement, when remarkable individuals pushed back the boundaries of what could be said and done. The boulevard realism of *La Ronde*, the celestial vistas of Mahler's symphonies, the simplicity of Loos's Michaelerplatz house and the gold-encrusted paintings of Klimt do not belong to any single 'movement'. In each case, however, the idea of what art could represent, or of what constituted its proper language of expression, was being challenged. That was certainly true of *La Ronde*, as Schnitzler was acutely aware.

La Ronde: What Happens in the Play

La Ronde consists of ten self-contained scenes. There are two
characters in each – a man and a woman. One of them
appears again in the next scene, with a different partner. The
tenth and final scene completes the cycle, with the return of
one of the characters from the first scene.

The play is set in and around the Vienna of its time. One scene
takes place in a country inn not far from the capital; the rest
are located in various places, some public, some private, in the
city. Some are quite specific and would have been familiar to
anyone living in Vienna. Many actual place-names,
establishments and well-known haunts are mentioned. Other
scenes are set in private houses and apartments, precisely
described in Schnitzler's meticulous stage directions and
representing certain characteristic, and socially specific, types.

1.   *The Prostitute* picks up *The Soldier*, offering him sex for free;
he refuses to go home with her, so they have sex by the river.
He has to get back to barracks and refuses to tell her his name.
He laughs off her request for a tip.

2.   *The Soldier* has led *The Maid* out of a dance hall on a
Sunday evening. They hardly know each other but soon go and
have sex in the park. He quickly loses interest in her and wants
to get back to the dance, but she prevaricates, asking if he is
fond of her. His reluctant promise to walk her home is soon
forgotten as he finds a new dancing partner.

3.   A hot summer's afternoon. *The Young Master* has been left
alone in the house and seduces *The Maid*. She is worried that they
might be interrupted, and he is concerned about the imminent
visit of Dr Schüller. They have sex; she asks him to stay, but he
leaves for the café. As soon as he's gone she steals a cigar.

4. *The Young Master* has borrowed an apartment for an assignation with *The Young Wife*. She appears thickly veiled, very anxious, and uttering all the clichés of the tempted wife. He pretends that the apartment is his, and she allows herself to be seduced. However, he suffers a bout of impotence for which he makes grandiose excuses. She mocks and teases him; a second attempt at sex is more successful. Unnerved by the prospect of the lies she is going to have to tell her husband, she declares that she will never see him again. But they are attending the same ball the following night and will meet there.

5. Late evening. *The Young Wife* is in bed. *The Husband* comes in and tells her that he still loves her and that the time has come once again for them to be more than 'just good friends'. He explains that their repeated periods of sexual abstinence mean that they keep having 'honeymoons'. She starts to ask him about the women he slept with before they were married and wonders if married women ever prostitute themselves. Having made love, he recalls the first night of their honeymoon in Venice, secure in the (false) knowledge of her fidelity.

6. *The Husband* is having dinner with *The Sweet Young Thing* in the private room of a restaurant. She is both flirtatious and innocent, and he wants to know everything about her – especially how promiscuous she is. She swoons – declaring that someone must have drugged her wine – and they have sex. She is desperate to know if he loves her, and wants to see him again. He says that he doesn't live in Vienna and packs her off home to her mother.

7. *The Sweet Young Thing* visits *The Poet's* room. It is dark but he refuses to light the lamps. He claims that he loves her and asks if she loves him in return. After having sex he says that he is Biebitz, a famous playwright (of whom she has never heard); then he informs her that he is only a shop assistant who plays the piano in a bar. She is bewildered, and he invites her to see

Biebitz's latest, declaring 'I'll only really know you, when I know what you think about the play.'

8.   *The Poet* (who really *is* Biebitz) is with a famous *Actress* in a country inn 'two hours from Vienna'. She keeps wrong-footing him by declaring her passion for him, but also her devotion to a man called Fritz. She says that she is going to bed without him but, moments later, invites him to join her. She taunts him with who she is betraying and they have sex. He is upset that she didn't perform in his play; she replies that she was ill, sick with longing for him.

9.   *The Count*, a cavalry officer, is paying a visit to *The Actress*. It is mid-morning, but she is still in bed, recuperating from some (imagined) indisposition. He says he was enchanted by her performance the previous night, and she flirts with him. He expounds his bleakly hedonistic view of life and tells her that he finds it difficult to be happy, even after having been posted back to Vienna. She teases him about his mistress. When she offers herself, he at first declines, pleading an aversion to sex in the mornings. But he soon succumbs and promises to return after her performance that evening.

10.   *The Count* wakes up on a sofa in the squalid room of *The Prostitute*. She is in bed, still asleep. He can remember almost nothing of the drunken night before. When she wakes, he questions her about her life. Her eyes reminds him of someone from his past; he tells her that she could have made a fortune, but she seems content with her lot. His romantic delusions are punctured when he learns that they had sex before he passed out. He leaves as another day dawns over Vienna.

La Ronde: Sex and Society

Schnitzler's play takes both its title and its structure from the roundelay or round-dance – perhaps the most basic and ancient of folk-dances, in which alternate boys and girls join hands to form a circle. The French know it as *la ronde*, the Germans as *der Reigen*. The dance is a primal and universal symbol of the earth, the circle of the seasons, and the cycle of life. It has sexual connotations, subversive of the idea of sexual fidelity to a single partner: for each boy is linked to two girls, and each girl to two boys. But it also has cultural associations with death: the mediaeval allegory of the *danse macabre* takes the form of the round-dance in which high and low, rich and poor caper together to the grave. This juxtaposition of sex and death is at the heart of the play.

Schnitzler once observed that 'what lies at the deepest level of human nature is the fear of death' – a primal instinct more profound even than the sexual desire that apparently brings the characters in *La Ronde* together. Though they talk of love, it is not love that they seek ('Love is, in fact, always a symbol for something else,' Schnitzler noted in his diary in 1895); nor, in the end, is it even sex itself. As the illusions of romance are stripped away, what is left is hunger for connection, for a moment of intensity which is also a moment of oblivion. As Schnitzler's characters grope blindly for each other, they are really trying to stave off death – yet they seem to sense that, in that very act, they are merely taking one more step towards the grave. Preoccupied with the passing of time, they are constantly asking or reminding each other what the time is and anxious at the unexpected lateness of the hour; the fading or dimming of daylight, and the gathering of darkness, is another recurring motif. Death also stalks the play in the form of the unspoken fear of syphilis (still incurable in the 1890s): 'God knows what kind of girl she is – Dear God . . . it was all so quick . . . not very careful of me' is the Husband's first thought after sex with the Sweet Young Thing. We are reminded how few degrees of separation stand between the top and bottom of society, and of the potentially fatal permeability of barriers of class, wealth and marital fidelity.

Schnitzler wrote in his diary on 25 March 1895:

> With M[i]z[zi] R[einhard], at our usual place. Some of it
> was amazing; the rest of the time she went on at me for
> no reason, until she had to get dressed and leave. When
> she'd gone, I broke down and wept at the sadness and
> littleness of it all, and how these things are really the
> seeds of slow and certain death. Death is certain, all
> right; you've just got to remember that, even in the first
> full bloom of a new affair – you can feel him sitting
> there. Because each relationship carries its death right
> from birth, just as people do.

Sex stands as a surrogate for death in *La Ronde*: the great
leveller, the common denominator. It is, in the full sense of the
word, a consummation, like death itself – the thing to which
everything the characters do and say ultimately leads. In a play
which is all talk, the only thing that *happens* is the sex. When all
the lying and verbal jousting ends, and there is nothing more to
be said, Schnitzler's text has a row of mute dots.

One can detect in Schnitzler's art – as in that of his near
contemporary and fellow doctor, Anton Chekhov (1860-1904) –
the writer as man of science, observing humanity in all its
frailty. Its combination of unflinching objectivity, empathetic
humanity and seen-it-all tolerance is rather like the perfect
bedside manner. But *La Ronde* also has something of the
anatomy lesson about it. We observe (and sometimes wince) as
the tissue of pretence is peeled back and the inner organs are
laid bare. The characters are left with nothing to hide. Every
lie, every self-deception is dissected. Like voyeurs, we watch two
people at their most intimate and their most exposed.

Ten Dialogues is the work's subtitle, and there is significance in
Schnitzler's choice of the term. Ever since Plato and the *Socratic
Dialogues*, this literary form has had pedagogic connotations.

The play's subtitle signals that this is no mere entertainment, but something from which we may learn: that these dialogues are to be treated as *exempla*. They are reminiscent of the case studies that Freud and Breuer published in 1895 in the seminal *Studies in Hysteria*. To borrow from Freud, one might even describe *La Ronde* as a study in the psychopathology of everyday life.

Freud's gruelling self-analysis formed the basis for all his later work; a similar spirit of self-experimentation seems to have motivated Schnitzler's candid journals. They are the product not so much of a confessional diarist as of a conscientious clinician keeping a careful note, and (as in the examples above) one can see in them the raw materials of his art. Freud got to the heart of this when he remarked in a letter to Schnitzler in 1922: 'It seems to me that you have learned through intuition – *or rather, from sensitive introspection* – everything that I have had to unearth by laborious work on other people' (emphasis added).

Certainly a remarkable product of 'sensitive introspection', *La Ronde* is also a portrait of an entire society. It is delineated by that characteristic literary figure of the nineteenth-century metropolis, the writer who observes the teeming life of the streets and cafés with the familiarity of the *habitué* and the curiosity of the social anthropologist: what the poet Charles Baudelaire (1821-1867) called 'the painter of modern life'. This tradition begins with Honoré de Balzac (1799-1850) and his *Comédie Humaine*, the cycle of realist novels written in the 1830s and 1840s, whose cross-section of society reminds us how close the *salon* can be to the gutter. It continues with Charles Dickens (1812-70); and in the finely-wrought prose of Gustav Flaubert (1821-80), from whose *Madame Bovary* (1856) Schnitzler mischievously borrows the names of Emma and her cuckold husband, Charles (Karl), for the bourgeois couple in *La Ronde*. Its modernist and reformist tendencies are emphasised in the naturalism of the novels of Émile Zola (1840-1902), with their portrayal of harsh lives of the Parisian working class; while the *boulevardier* novellas and tales of Guy de Maupassant (1850-1893), the plays and short stories of Chekhov and the great cycle of naturalist dramas of Henrik Ibsen (1828-1906) reveal the currents of anxiety, repression and hypocrisy beneath the placid surface of bourgeois life.

La Ronde is a late and consciously daring product of that humanistic, liberal and realist tradition, with which Schnitzler identified and to which he belonged. The world of the play is not that of the Viennese cultural avant-garde in which Schnitzler himself moved, but its antithesis: low, high or middling, these are the ordinary people of the metropolis, oblivious to the artistic and cultural innovations going on around them. Even the Poet seems unaware of it all: evidently third-rate, he spouts pseudo-Symbolist nonsense. Though these characters are driven by their sexual appetites, they are not presented as being especially promiscuous, and certainly not as depraved.

Theatrical censorship was the norm throughout Europe in the 1890s (and remained so for many decades beyond). Any allusion on stage to sexual activity was banned; the actual depiction of it, unimaginable. In that cultural context, 'avant-garde' would be a fair way to characterise a play about ten acts of copulation, mostly casual and all but one outside marriage. It is not surprising that early critical reaction to *La Ronde* – in the relatively few instances where the work was not condemned as an affront to public decency – focused on how radical a departure it represented (see 'The Struggle for Acceptance', below). But the play's modernity has deep roots, stretching back to the liberal, secular tradition of literary realism of the mid-nineteenth century; to the sceptical rationalism of the eighteenth century; and arguably, all the way to the scientific revolution of the century before.

The idea of 'decadence' has traditionally been associated with the culture (especially the avant-garde culture) of *fin-de-siècle*

Vienna, with *La Ronde* sometimes held out as the prime
example. But 'decadence' is not so much a feature of this
avant-garde as a critique of it. Commentators for whom
Schnitzler's generation of artists represented a threat (to taste,
decency or social order) frequently labelled them as decadent –
as embodying a 'falling-off'. Those hostile to the idea that
human beings could be at the mercy of their unconscious
desires, or that sexuality had its roots in early childhood,
similarly dismissed Freud's theories as 'decadent'. Indeed, the
words 'decadent' and 'Jewish' were often paired, invariably with
hostile intent. The brush once used to tar everything of which
those who wielded it disapproved is not likely to be a useful
instrument now, even in sympathetic hands.

More recently, the idea of Viennese 'decadence' has been
replaced by a preoccupation with 'pessimism' – the notion that
this was a civilisation which foresaw, even somehow willed, its
undoing. This is a generalisation of doubtful value, born of
hindsight. On the other hand, much (though by no means all)
of the art of the period undoubtedly does manifest a sense of
anxiety, foreboding, or unrest. There is something of this in *La
Ronde*, too: Schnitzler wrote the play as he emerged from a
period of personal crisis and desolation, and the work reflects
his own feelings, around this time, of the hopelessness of love
and of the impossibility of truthful relations between men and
women. But to call the play gloomy or nihilistic would be wide
of the mark. Its tone is predominantly light, satirical and even
playful. It is comedic not just in form, but most of the time also
in its content – even if the laughs are generally at the expense
of the characters (especially the male characters). Schnitzler is
too entertained by the sheer humanity of these people, with
their endless capacity to deceive themselves and each other, for
the play to be bleak. The tone is richly ironic, and the dialogue
crackles with the thrust-and-parry of men and women trying
deftly to outmanoeuvre each other in expressive everyday

language. Though *La Ronde* tells some unpalatable truths, there is not a trace of misanthropy (still less of misogyny) about it.

That the play was condemned as 'pornographic' by the cultural reactionaries of early twentieth-century Austria and Germany tells us something about those societies, but very little about the work itself. There was undoubtedly a particular fascination in late nineteenth-century culture in Vienna (as elsewhere) with sexuality and ideas of deviancy and perversity – from the fetishist fantasies of Leopold von Sacher-Masoch (1836-1905) in his novel *Venus in Furs* (1869), through the *Psychopathia Sexualis* (1886) of Richard Krafft-Ebing (1840-1902), to the groundbreaking work of Freud himself on infantile sexuality. But the charge of pornography does not stick to *La Ronde*. The play is distinctly *anti*-erotic – dealing, as it does, with the halting run-ups to and the deflated comings-down from actual sex. Indeed, theatrical tradition has been to lower the curtain or have a blackout during the passages indicated by a row of dots.

La Ronde: the Struggle for Acceptance

Few plays have caused as much controversy as *La Ronde*, and the story of its struggle for acceptance is worth recounting.

Schnitzler wrote the play in the winter of 1896-7; two days after finishing it, he commented in a letter that 'it is quite unprintable, of not much literary importance, but, dug up after a few hundred years, might throw unique light on part of our culture'. He sent the manuscript to the Berlin theatre critic Alfred Kerr, who cautiously advised him to publish but to replace the original title, *Ein Liebesreigen* ('A Round Dance of Love'), with the simpler *Reigen* ('Round Dance'). Schnitzler's usual publisher, the distinguished Berlin house of S. Fischer Verlag, declined the work, fearing repercussions. In 1900 Schnitzler had it privately printed, distributing 200 copies among friends and colleagues with a clear indication that it was not to be performed. The play finally received commercial publication (with a few amendments) on 2 April 1903 by Wiener Verlag; the edition sold 40,000 copies.

Despite popular acclaim, most critics expressed disapproval ('nothing but filth', said the *Neue Bahnen*), some dismissing the work as pornography. The right-wing press was predictably hostile, adding anti-Semitic insult to injury. Disregarding Schnitzler's insistence that *La Ronde* should not be performed, the drama society of Munich University presented three of the dialogues (the fifth, sixth and seventh) in Munich on 25 June 1903. The production was well attended and politely received; the press reaction was, once again, almost entirely negative, one critic dismissing it as 'hostile to culture'. This prompted further widespread commentary, largely from journalists and politicians who had not seen the performance. The university was eventually forced to take action and closed down the drama society.

A public reading of the play in Vienna was announced for 8 November 1903, which the authorities promptly banned; a literary society in Breslau (now Wrocław) held a reading later that month. In March 1904, the Berlin public prosecutor had copies of the book confiscated, and in September two booksellers offering it were prosecuted for selling pornography. They were acquitted, but further sales in Germany were banned. Private readings were given in Berlin in 1905 and 1909.

Schnitzler entrusted the play's Hungarian translation to the dramatist Sándor Bródy; this was published in Budapest in 1904 under the imprint of Wiener Verlag's owner, Fritz Freund. On 13 October 1912 a small avant-garde Budapest theatre, the Uj Szinpad, gave the first full staging of the whole play, in Bródy's translation, directed by Albert Kövessy. The authorities banned it after a single performance.

Reports reached Schnitzler of unlicensed performances in
Moscow and St Petersburg in early 1917, and of Austrian
prisoners-of-war acting scenes from the play in a Russian camp.
In November 1918, the great Austrian director Max Reinhardt
approached Schnitzler for permission to stage *La Ronde* in
Berlin. After much delay, but persuaded of the seriousness of
Reinhardt's intentions, he finally agreed. However, Reinhardt
resigned in the summer of 1920, and the production was
entrusted to the highly-regarded Austrian director Hubert
Reusch. The premiere was announced for 23 December 1920
in the Kleines Schauspielhaus. A few hours before curtain-up,
the music academy from whom the theatre was leased obtained
an injunction against performance on the grounds of the play's
immorality; this was ignored and the premiere went ahead, to
mostly favourable reviews. The injunction was lifted on 6
January 1921 with the judges, who had attended a
performance, calling the work a 'moral deed'. On 22 February
1921, protestors stormed the theatre. The public prosecutor's
office investigated and, after concerted lobbying from influential
opponents of the play, brought proceedings for offences of
public indecency against Reusch, the cast and the theatre
managers. The defence marshalled a notable array of expert
witnesses at the six-day trial, which resulted in the acquittal of
all thirteen defendants on 18 November 1921.

Meanwhile, on 1 February 1921, *La Ronde* had been presented
at the Deutsches Volkstheater in Vienna: Schnitzler had
monitored rehearsals and the first performance went off
without protest. Some of the press praised the play's artistic
content but objected to the fact that such explicit scenes were
being performed in public; the right-wing papers, however,
denounced it, urging readers to make their feelings known.
Several performances were interrupted by violent protestors
and, in 16 February 1921, a mob of some 600 wrecked the
theatre. The following day the police forbade any further

performances. The Austrian government supported this move and ordered the Social Democrat mayor to follow suit; this was soon declared unconstitutional, and stormy scenes in parliament ensued, including a failed attempt to impeach the mayor. Performances resumed on 7 March 1922, in a theatre bristling with police. Productions elsewhere in Europe in 1922 each gave rise to protest and controversy, and from that year on, Schnitzler refused all requests for public performance rights.

The first translation of *La Ronde* into English was by F.L. Glaser and the anonymous 'L.D.E'; authorised by Schnitzler, it was published in New York under the title *Hands Around: A Cycle of Ten Dialogues* in 1920 in an edition of 1,475 copies 'privately printed for subscribers' and 'intended for private circulation only'. It was performed in England in 1923 in a private house belonging to members of the liberal-minded Bloomsbury group. Virginia Woolf wrote that 'the audience felt simply as if a real copulation were going on in the room and tried to drown the very realistic moans . . . ' An American production planned for March 1923 in New York was shelved when objections were raised. In October 1926, it was staged without incident at the Triangle Theatre Club in New York; but the city's anti-vice campaigners tirelessly harried booksellers who stocked the work, finally obtaining a conviction in 1929 under the obscenity laws.

The Nazis labelled Schnitzler a Jewish pornographer and 'degenerate'; on coming to power in Germany in 1933, they banned his entire works and destroyed what copies they could lay their hands on.

Schnitzler's estate continued to refuse permission to stage *La Ronde* until 1981, when the fiftieth anniversary of his death took it out of copyright. The following year saw numerous revivals (some with just two performers) in Austria, Britain and elsewhere in Europe. Although the play is not often staged today, it has been accepted as a defining work of *fin-de-siècle*

Vienna, with the controversies that accompanied it seen as an important chapter in the artist's struggle for free expression.

Three films have been based on the play. Max Ophüls' celebrated adaptation *La Ronde* (1950) starred Simone Signoret, Gérard Philippe and Jean-Louis Barrault; hailed as a masterpiece, the film takes considerable liberties with Schnitzler's text and now seems rather far in spirit from the original. In 1964, Roger Vadim set the action in Paris just before the First World War, with mixed results. In 1973, the Viennese theatre and opera director Otto Schenk directed *Reigen* in a strikingly faithful and handsome original-language film version, with a cast that included Maria Schneider and Helmut Lohner.

More recently, there have been several 'radical' theatrical adaptations. Eric Bentley's homosexual version *Round 2* was performed in 1990; David Hare's play *The Blue Room* (1998), inspired by Schnitzler but set in 'a modern city', was directed by Sam Mendes and presented in London and New York with Nicole Kidman and Iain Glen; and Michael John La Chiusa's musical *Hello Again* in 1994, and Jack Heifner's 2004 play *Seduction,* both took the play as inspiration.

A Note on the Text

Any translator of *La Ronde* is faced with the question of which text to use. We have drawn both on the 1896-7 original version (*Ein Liebesreigen*), the manuscript of which is in the Bibliotheca Bodmeriana in Geneva (and published in Gabriella Rovagnati, *Ein Liebesreigen: Die Urfassung des 'Reigen'*, 2004), and the 1903 Wiener Verlag edition. It is clear that most of the (generally minor) amendments were made with the aim of toning down the play's sexual explicitness, especially as regards the female characters. Living in more robust times, we have almost always preferred the unexpurgated original.

One of our first decisions was the title and here, sadly, English doesn't help: *Round Dance* has none of the right associations, and we wanted to avoid a radical renaming. Perhaps in deference to Ophüls' great film, we have decided that the French title *La Ronde* is the best.

We see the play as being of its time and place and have kept most of the proper names in their original form. The modulations in Schnitzler's text between *Sie* and *du* (respectively, the formal and intimate forms of 'you') are highly significant; we have had to make do with various indirect ways of indicating these shifts, such as introducing terms of endearment as a substitute. None of these devices is entirely satisfactory, but we feel that they are preferable to simply ignoring the point. On the whole, we have not retained the distinctively Austrian formalities of address, such as *küss die Hand* ('[I] kiss your hand'), except where some equivalent English expression was available. Generally, we have tried to find a palette of tones which reflect the minute twists and turns of Schnitzler's brilliantly heard, class-specific dialogue. We have not attempted a pastiche of Edwardian English, although we have done our best to avoid obvious anachronisms. Above all, we have sought to achieve speakable, idiomatic English which captures the spirit, rather than always the absolute letter, of the original.

We are grateful to the remarkable group of actors who read a draft of this translation in the rehearsal room of English Touring Theatre in March 2007. The acid test of any dialogue is to hear it spoken aloud, and the actors helped sharpen our ears; where we have failed, the fault is entirely our own.

Stephen Unwin, Peter Zombory-Moldovan
London, October 2007

For Further Reading

Several English translations of the play are available. F.L. Glaser's 1920 translation, *Hands Around*, was reprinted in Dover Thrift Editions. A fine, racy translation by Marya Mannes was published in New York in 1933 by The Modern Library. Eric Bentley's 1954 translation was published by Samuel French. Three versions appeared in 1982: Methuen published a translation by Frank Marcus; the director John Barton adapted it for the Royal Shakespeare Company, from a literal translation by Sue Davies; and Carcanet Press published Charles Osborne's new version, *The Round Dance*. J.M.Q. Davies' *Round Dance* for Oxford World's Classics (2004) is a solid academic account, equipped with invaluable notes and an excellent introduction by Ritchie Robertson.

Schnitzler's novels are increasingly available in English: Pushkin Press has recently published handsome editions of *Fräulein Else*, *Casanova's Return to Venice* and *Dying*, and Penguin has published *Dream Story*. Schnitzler's autobiography was published in English in 1970 as *My Youth in Vienna*.

Carl E. Schorske's *Fin-de-Siècle Vienna: Politics and Culture* (1980) and Steven Beller's *Vienna and the Jews 1867-1938: A Cultural History* (1989) provide valuable insights into Schnitzler's cultural milieu. Especially pertinent, though its canvas is wider, is Peter Gay's *Schnitzler's Century: The Making of Middle-Class Culture 1815-1914* (2001).

Arthur Schnitzler: Key Dates

1862   15 May: born in Vienna.

1871-9 Attends the Akademisches Gymnasium, Vienna. Passes
final exams with honours. Enrols at the University of
Vienna to study medicine.

1882-3 Military service as a medical assistant.

1885   Graduates; starts work as intern and assistant doctor at
the university teaching hospital.

1886-8 Publication of his poems and aphorisms in the *Deutsche
Wochenschrift* and *An der schönen blauen Donau*, as well as
medical articles in the *Wienere Medizinische Presse* and the
Internationale Klinische Rundschau.

1888   Visits Berlin and London for study. Becomes assistant to
his father at the Allgemeine Wiener Poliklinik.

1889   Publication of his medical treatise *On Functional Aphonia
and its Treatment through Hypnosis and Suggestion*. Begins
relationship with Marie Glümer.

1892   Publication of the one-act play cycle *Anatol*.

1893   Death of his father. Resigns from the Poliklinik and
starts a private practice. Premieres of the one-act play
Farewell Supper (from *Anatol*) in Bad Ischl and *The Fairy
Tale* at the Deutsches Volkstheater, Vienna. Begins
relationship with the actress Adéle Sandrock.

1894   Begins relationship with Marie Reinhard, one of his
patients. Onset of deafness and tinnitus. Publication of

1907   Publication of the Collected Novellas: *Souls in Twilight*.

1908   Publication of the novel *The Way Out Into the Open*.

1909   Premiere of the one-act play *Countess Mitzi* at the
Deutsches Volkstheater, Vienna. Birth of daughter Lili.

1910   Buys a large house in Vienna in which he lives until his
death.

1911   Death of his mother. Premiere of *The Vast Domain* at the
Burgtheater, Vienna, and various German theatres.

1912   Publication of *Collected Works* in two parts. Premiere
of *Professor Bernhardi* at the Kleines Theater, Berlin.
Premiere of *La Ronde* (in Hungarian) at the Uj Szinpad,
Budapest.

1913   Publication of the novella *Frau Beate and her Son*.

1915   Premiere of the cycle of one-act plays *Comedy of Words*
in Vienna, Darmstadt and Frankfurt.

1918   Publication of the novella *The Return of Casanova*.
Austrian premiere of *Professor Bernhardi* at the Deutsches
Volkstheater, Vienna.

1920   23 December: premiere of *La Ronde* (in German) at the
Kleines Schauspielhaus, Berlin.

1921   1 February: Austrian premiere of *La Ronde* in the
Kammerspiele of the Deutsches Volkstheater, Vienna.
17 February: Performances of *La Ronde* in Vienna
prohibited as 'a threat to law and order'. November:
Trial in Berlin and acquittal of the director, actors and
management of the Kleines Schauspielhaus. Divorces
Olga.

1922   March: The ban in Germany on *La Ronde* is lifted.

1924   Premiere of *Comedy of Seduction* at the Burgtheater,
        Vienna. Publication of the short story *Fräulein Else*.

1925-6 Publication of the novel *Dream Story*.

1927   Publication of *Book of Maxims and Doubts, Aphorisms and
        Fragments*.

1928   Lili, his daughter, commits suicide. Publication of the
        novel *Therese: A Chronicle of a Woman's Life*.

1929   Premiere of *Wafted by Summer Breezes* at the Deutsches
        Volkstheater, Vienna.

1931   Premiere of *The Walk to the Fish Pond* at the Burgtheater,
        Vienna. Publication of the novel *Flight into Darkness*.
        21 October: dies.

LA RONDE

Ten Dialogues

Characters

PROSTITUTE
SOLDIER
MAID
YOUNG MASTER
YOUNG WIFE
HUSBAND
SWEET YOUNG THING
POET
ACTRESS
COUNT

1. The Prostitute and the Soldier

Late evening. By the Augarten Bridge. The SOLDIER *enters, whistling, on his way home.*

PROSTITUTE. Come on, handsome.

He turns, then keeps walking.

D'you want some company?

SOLDIER. Me? Handsome?

PROSTITUTE. Course. Who else? Come on, I'm just up the road.

SOLDIER. Ain't got time. Got to get back to barracks.

PROSTITUTE. You'll get back to barracks all right. Better at my place, though.

SOLDIER (*closer*). Maybe.

PROSTITUTE. Ssh. A copper might turn up.

SOLDIER. Yeah, right. Like to see a copper deal with this.

Pats his bayonet-case.

PROSTITUTE. Come on then.

SOLDIER. Piss off. Anyway, I ain't got no money.

PROSTITUTE. Don't need any.

SOLDIER (*stops short. Under a street lamp*). No money? Who are you, anyway?

PROSTITUTE. Ordinary blokes pay. Soldiers like you get it for free.

SOLDIER. I bet you're the one Huber told me about.

PROSTITUTE. Never heard of him.

SOLDIER. You must be. You know – the café in the Schiffgasse – you went home with him.

PROSTITUTE. Wouldn't be the first from there. Mmm . . .

SOLDIER. Come on then. Come on.

PROSTITUTE. In a hurry now, are we?

SOLDIER. Well, what're we hanging about for? And I've got to be in barracks by ten.

PROSTITUTE. When did you join up, then?

SOLDIER. What's it matter to you? How far's your place?

PROSTITUTE. Ten minutes.

SOLDIER. That's too far. Give us a snog.

PROSTITUTE (*kisses him*). I always think that's the best bit. When I really fancy a bloke.

SOLDIER. Dunno 'bout that. Forget it, it's too far.

PROSTITUTE. Tell you what, come round tomorrow then. In the afternoon.

SOLDIER. All right. Give us your address.

PROSTITUTE. But you ain't gonna come, are you?

SOLDIER. I told you.

PROSTITUTE. Tell you what, if my place is too far – what about down there?

Towards the Danube.

SOLDIER. You what?

PROSTITUTE. It's quiet down there. No one about.

SOLDIER. Nah. Not my idea of a good time.

PROSTITUTE. I'll give you a good time, don't you worry about that. Come on, stay with me. Who knows, we could all be dead by tomorrow.

SOLDIER. All right. But hurry up.

PROSTITUTE. Watch out. It's dark. One slip, and you're in the river.

SOLDIER. Best place for me.

PROSTITUTE. Afterwards, maybe ... Hey, slow down a bit. There's a bench just ahead.

SOLDIER. You know your way around.

PROSTITUTE. I could do with someone like you.

SOLDIER. You couldn't handle me.

PROSTITUTE. I could have fun trying.

SOLDIER. Ha ha.

PROSTITUTE. Keep it down. Coppers come wandering round even down here sometimes. Wouldn't think it, would you: here we are, right in the middle of the city.

SOLDIER. Come here. Come on.

PROSTITUTE. Careful, or we'll both be in the river.

SOLDIER (*has got hold of her*). Oh yeah.

PROSTITUTE. Hold on tight.

SOLDIER. Don't you worry ... ah ...

• •

PROSTITUTE. Would have been better on the bench.

SOLDIER. Who cares? Come on, get up.

PROSTITUTE. What's the rush?

SOLDIER. Got to get to barracks. I'm late.

PROSTITUTE. So what's your name, then?

SOLDIER. What do you care?

PROSTITUTE. I'm Leocadia.

SOLDIER. Uh! That's a new one.

PROSTITUTE. Hey ... I want to tell you something ... you were so good ... so ... ooh ... so ... come here ...

SOLDIER. You've got to be kidding.

PROSTITUTE. Hey.

SOLDIER. What is it now?

PROSTITUTE. At least gimme sixpence for the housekeeper.

SOLDIER. Huh! What sort of a sucker do you think I am? See you, 'Leocadia'.

PROSTITUTE. You scum! Bastard!

He's gone.

2. The Soldier and the Maid

The Prater. Sunday evening. A path leading from the Wurstelprater towards a dark avenue of trees. The distant sounds of the amusement park; and the 'Five-Kreutzer Polka', a corny dance tune, played by a brass band.

MAID. Go on, tell me. Why do you have to go so early?

The SOLDIER *is embarrassed, and laughs stupidly.*

It was lovely. I love dancing.

He holds the MAID *around the waist. She lets him.*

We're not dancing now. Why are you holding me so tight?

SOLDIER. What was your name again? Kathi, isn't it?

MAID. You've got some Kathi on the brain.

SOLDIER. Oh, yeah, I know: Marie.

MAID. It's getting dark. Spooky.

SOLDIER. You got nothing to worry about. You're with me. I'll look after you.

MAID. What are we doing out here? All on our own. Come on, let's go back inside. It's all dark out here.

SOLDIER (*draws on his cigar, making the end glow*). There, that's lit things up!

Laughs.

Hello, gorgeous!

MAID. Hey, what are you doing? I might have known . . .

SOLDIER. Damn, if yours aren't the nicest handful in there tonight.

MAID. Tested all the rest, then, have you?

SOLDIER. You can tell, dancing with someone. Quite a lot you can tell that way, wouldn't you say?

MAID. But you was dancing with that blonde a lot more than you was with me. That squinty one.

SOLDIER. Friend of a friend, you might say.

MAID. What, that corporal with the twirly moustache?

SOLDIER. No, my friend was the civvy: you know, he was sat next to me, the bloke with a croaky voice.

MAID. Oh, him. He's got a bloody nerve.

SOLDIER. What'd he do to you? I'll show him. What'd he do?

MAID. Oh, nothing. Just how he was with the other girls.

SOLDIER. So tell me, Marie.

MAID. Watch it with that cigar, will you?

SOLDIER. Sorry. Marie. Come here, darling.

MAID. You're being a bit familiar, aren't you?

SOLDIER. Don't you like me calling you darling? Come on, it's just an expression ...

MAID. Bit soon for that, isn't it? Now then, Franz ...

SOLDIER. You remember my name, then?

MAID. Course I do, Franz ...

SOLDIER. The lads call me Franzi. And the girls, too ...

MAID. Steady on. What if someone was to come out?

SOLDIER. So what if they do? They'll never see us.

MAID. Where are you taking me?

SOLDIER. Hey, look, a couple over there, just like us.

MAID. Where? I can't see a thing.

SOLDIER. There. Straight ahead.

MAID. What do you mean, just like us?

SOLDIER. Well, they're just being friendly too.

MAID. Careful, what's this? I nearly fell over it.

SOLDIER. Just the railings round the grass.

MAID. Stop that pushing, will you, or you'll have me on the ground.

SOLDIER. Sshh. Not so loud.

MAID. Look, I'm going to shout at you in a minute . . . What are you up to? Hey?

SOLDIER. We've got the place to ourselves.

MAID. Let's go back and join the others.

SOLDIER. We don't need them, Marie, all we need is . . . uh . . .

MAID. But Franz, please, Jesus, look, if I'd known . . . oh . . . yes.

• •

SOLDIER (*in bliss*). Christ almighty . . . ah . . .

MAID. I can't see your face.

SOLDIER. Never mind my face . . .

• •

SOLDIER. Come on, Marie, you can't just lie there.

MAID. Well, give us a hand then, Franzi.

SOLDIER. There you go.

MAID. Oh God. Franzi.

SOLDIER. What have I done now?

MAID. You're a bad man ... Franzi.

SOLDIER. Yeah. Hang on a sec.

MAID. Why d'you let go of me?

SOLDIER. Let me get this thing (*the cigar*) lit, can't you?

MAID. It's so dark.

SOLDIER. Be light again in the morning.

MAID. Just tell me, do you ... like me?

SOLDIER. What'd it feel like?

Laughs.

MAID. Where're we going now?

SOLDIER. Back inside, where d'you think?

MAID. In a minute. Please.

SOLDIER. What's up now? I ain't hanging about in the dark all night.

MAID. Come on, Franzi, tell me if you like me.

SOLDIER. I just said, didn't I?

MAID. Will you give me a kiss?

SOLDIER (*gracious*). There. Listen. There's the music again.

MAID. Do you just want to go on dancing now?

SOLDIER. Sure. What's wrong with that?

MAID. Look, Franzi, it's just that I've got to get back. My missus will give me hell, she's such a ... She'd rather I never went out at all.

SOLDIER. All right. Go home, then.

MAID. I just thought you might walk me home.

SOLDIER. Walk you home, eh?

MAID. It's just a bit lonely, walking home at night all on your own. Go on.

SOLDIER. Where is it you live, then?

MAID. Not far. Porzellangasse.

SOLDIER. Well, I s'pose it's on my way ... but it's too early for me. I've got a few more dances in me yet. I've got the whole night ... I don't have to be back at barracks till midnight. I'm going to go on dancing.

MAID. Oh, I get it. It's Squinty Blonde's turn now, is it?

SOLDIER. She's not that bad.

MAID. God, men are such bastards. I suppose you do this with every girl.

SOLDIER. I couldn't manage them all.

MAID. Oh please, Franzi, not tonight. Just me tonight. Stay with me. Please ...

SOLDIER. Yeah, yeah, all right. But I can have a couple more dances, can't I?

MAID. I'm not doing any more dancing tonight!

SOLDIER. And there it is.

MAID. What?

SOLDIER. The dance hall. Didn't take us long. And it's that tune again ...

Singing along.

Ta da ra da, ta da ra da. Look, if you want to wait for me, I'll see you home. Or I'll see ya. Up to you.

MAID. All right, I'll wait.

They enter the dance hall.

SOLDIER. Look, Marie, why don't you get yourself a beer?

Turning to a blonde who is just dancing past with a young man. All formal.

Would you care for a dance?

3. The Maid and the Young Master

*Hot summer afternoon. His parents have left for the country. The cook is
on her day off. The* MAID *is in the kitchen, writing to the Soldier. The
bell from the* YOUNG MASTER*'s room rings. She gets up and goes
through to his room. He is lying on a divan, smoking and reading a French
novel.*

MAID. You rang, sir?

YOUNG MASTER. Oh, yes, Marie, so I did ... Now, what
was it ... ? Oh, yes, I know, pull the blinds down, would
you. It's cooler with the blinds down ... hm.

*She goes to the window and pulls down the roller-blind. He goes on
reading.*

What are you doing? Oh, yes, of course. But now there's not
enough light to read.

MAID. Oh, sir, you study too much.

YOUNG MASTER (*graciously letting it pass*). Yes ... mm ...

*She leaves. He tries to continue reading. Soon drops the book and rings
again. She returns.*

Oh, Marie ... Yes, now, what was I going to say? Ah,
yes ... Is there any brandy?

MAID. Yes, sir, but it'll be locked away.

YOUNG MASTER. So who's got the keys?

MAID. Lini has the keys.

YOUNG MASTER. Who's Lini?

MAID. You know, sir, the cook.

YOUNG MASTER. Well, go and ask Lini, then.

MAID. Yes, but it's her day off.

YOUNG MASTER. I see.

MAID. Shall I nip over to the café for you?

YOUNG MASTER. No, no. I'm hot enough already, as it is. I don't really want any brandy. Tell you what, though, Marie: bring me a glass of water, will you? And, um, Marie, let the tap run so it's nice and cool, eh?

She leaves. He watches her go. At the door she turns round and looks at him. He stares into space. She turns on the tap and lets it run. She goes to her little room, washes her hands and arranges her hair in the mirror. She fetches the water and goes over to the divan. He gets halfway up. She puts the glass in his hand and their fingers touch.

Oh, thank you . . . Well, what is it? . . . Careful: put it back on the tray.

He stretches on the divan.

What's the time, by the way?

MAID. Five o'clock, sir.

YOUNG MASTER. Five? Right . . .

She leaves. But at the door she turns. He has been watching. She notices and smiles. He lies still for a moment, and then suddenly gets up. He walks over to the door, goes back and lies down again. He tries to read. After a moment or two he rings. She enters with a smile which she doesn't try to hide.

Now, Marie, I know what I wanted to ask you: didn't Dr Schüller drop by this morning?

MAID. No. No one all morning.

YOUNG MASTER. That's odd. So Dr Schüller didn't call? You do know who I mean?

MAID. Of course. The tall gentleman. With the black beard.

YOUNG MASTER. That's him. Did he call, then?

MAID. No. There's been no one, sir.

YOUNG MASTER (*suddenly*). Marie, come over here.

MAID (*coming a bit closer*). Yes, sir?

YOUNG MASTER. Closer. That's right. I was, um, just thinking ...

MAID. Yes, sir?

YOUNG MASTER. I was just thinking ... I was just wondering ... your blouse ... What kind of, erm ... ? Why don't you come a bit closer, I won't bite.

MAID (*coming closer*). What's wrong with it, sir? Don't you like it?

YOUNG MASTER (*stretches out to feel the blouse, pulling her down close to him*). Is that blue ... ? What a lovely shade of blue.

Simply.

I like the way you're dressed, Marie.

MAID. Oh, sir.

YOUNG MASTER. What? ...

He has unbuttoned her blouse. Matter-of-fact.

You've got beautiful skin, Marie. So pale.

MAID. Oh, sir, you'll make me blush.

YOUNG MASTER (*kissing her breasts*). There. That didn't hurt, did it?

MAID. No, sir.

Sighs.

YOUNG MASTER. Listen to you! What's the matter?

MAID. Oh, Master Alfred.

YOUNG MASTER. And those sweet little shoes you've got on ...

MAID. But, sir ... someone might ring ...

YOUNG MASTER. Who's going to ring now?

MAID. But, sir ... it's broad daylight.

YOUNG MASTER. You needn't be shy in front of me. Or in front of anyone ... someone as pretty as you. Honestly, Marie, you're ... You know, even your hair smells wonderful.

MAID. Master Alfred.

YOUNG MASTER. Don't give me that, Marie ... I've seen you ... The other evening, when I came in late. I went out to the kitchen for a glass of water ... Your door was open, and ... the cover had slid off your bed ...

MAID (*covers her face*). God, I never thought you could be so –

YOUNG MASTER. And I saw you then, all right. I saw this, and this, and ... this ... and ...

MAID. Master Alfred ...

YOUNG MASTER. Come on ... here ... yes, like that ... that's right ...

MAID. But what if someone rings the doorbell ...

YOUNG MASTER. Stop fussing ... anyway, they can wait ...

• •

The doorbell rings.

YOUNG MASTER. Bloody hell ... What a racket. Maybe he rang earlier and we didn't hear.

MAID. Oh, I was listening out the whole time.

YOUNG MASTER. Well, go and have a look. Just through the peep-hole, mind.

MAID. Master Alfred, you're, so ... well, bad.

YOUNG MASTER. Just go and see who it is, will you.

She does herself up hurriedly and goes out. He quickly lets up the blinds.

MAID (*coming back*). Well, whoever it was, they've gone. No one there. It could have been Dr Schüller.

YOUNG MASTER (*disagreeable*). That'll be all.

She goes to him and he moves away.

Right, Marie, I'm off now. To the café –

MAID (*tenderly*). Couldn't you stay for a little while? It'd be so nice ...

YOUNG MASTER (*strictly*). I'm going to the café. If Dr Schüller calls ...

MAID. He's not coming back today.

YOUNG MASTER (*more strictly*). If Dr Schüller calls, I'll be ... in the café.

Goes. She takes a cigar from the table, puts it in her pocket and leaves.

4. The Young Master and the Young Wife

Evening. A sitting room in the Schwindgasse, elegantly but anonymously furnished. The YOUNG MASTER *has just come in and, with his hat and coat still on, lights the candles. Then he opens the door into the next room and looks in. The candles shine across the parquet floor to strike the four-poster bed against the back wall. The glow from the fireplace reddens the bed curtains. He inspects the bedroom. He gets perfume from the chest of drawers and sprays the pillows. Then he sprays it through both rooms, and the whole place smells of violets. He takes his hat and coat off. He sits down in a blue velvet armchair and lights a cigarette. After a pause, he gets up and checks that the green shutters are closed. Suddenly he goes back into the bedroom and opens the drawer of the dressing-table. He feels inside and finds a tortoiseshell comb. He looks for somewhere to hide it, and finally puts it in his coat pocket. Then he opens a cupboard in the sitting room, takes out a silver tray with a bottle of cognac and two liqueur glasses and puts them on the table. He goes back to his coat and takes out a small white box. He opens it and puts it beside the cognac, then goes back to the cupboard and gets two small plates and some cutlery. He picks a marron glacé from the box and eats it. He pours himself a glass of cognac and drinks it down in a gulp. Then he looks at his watch. He paces up and down. He stands for a while in front of the big wall mirror and combs his hair and moustache with his pocket-comb. He then goes to the door to the hallway and listens. Nothing. He closes the blue curtain in front of the bedroom door. The doorbell rings, and he is startled. Then he sits down in the armchair and only gets up when the door opens and the* YOUNG WIFE *enters, closing the door behind her. She is heavily veiled and stands there for a moment with her right hand to her breast, as if to control her emotions.*

YOUNG MASTER (*approaches her, takes her left hand and kisses her white glove with its black stitching. In a hushed voice*). Thank you.

YOUNG WIFE. Alfred. Oh, Alfred.

YOUNG MASTER. Do come in. Please, Emma, come in.

YOUNG WIFE. May I just . . . just for a moment . . . Please.
Oh, please Alfred.

She stays standing at the door. He stands in front of her, holding her hand.

Where am I? In fact?

YOUNG MASTER. At my place.

YOUNG WIFE. But this house is awful, Alfred.

YOUNG MASTER. What do you mean? It's very respectable.

YOUNG WIFE. I met two men on the stairs.

YOUNG MASTER. People you know?

YOUNG WIFE. Maybe. I couldn't tell.

YOUNG MASTER. Forgive me, but surely you'd know if you
knew them.

YOUNG WIFE. I couldn't see a thing.

YOUNG MASTER. Your closest friends wouldn't have
recognised you. Even I, if I hadn't known it was you . . . in
that veil.

YOUNG WIFE. Two veils.

YOUNG MASTER. Look, why don't you come in . . . and take
your hat off, at least.

YOUNG WIFE. Alfred, will you please behave yourself? I told
you: five minutes . . . Not a second longer, I swear –

YOUNG MASTER. What about your veil?

YOUNG WIFE. Two veils.

YOUNG MASTER. Both of your veils, then. – At least let me
see you.

YOUNG WIFE. Do you love me, Alfred?

YOUNG MASTER (*deeply hurt*). Emma, how can you ask?

YOUNG WIFE. It's so hot in here.

YOUNG MASTER. You've still got your fur coat on. Mind
you don't catch a cold.

YOUNG WIFE (*finally enters the room and throws herself into the
armchair*). I'm absolutely exhausted.

YOUNG MASTER. May I?

*He takes off her veils, removes the hatpin, places hat, pin and veils
beside each other on the sofa. She lets it happen. He stands in front of
her, shaking his head.*

YOUNG WIFE. What?

YOUNG MASTER. I've never seen you look so beautiful.

YOUNG WIFE. Really?

YOUNG MASTER. Just ... to be alone with you ... Emma ...

*He kneels beside the armchair, holds her hands and covers them with
kisses.*

YOUNG WIFE. And now let me go. I've done what you asked.

He drops his head into her lap.

You promised you'd behave.

YOUNG MASTER. Yes.

YOUNG WIFE. It's boiling in here.

YOUNG MASTER. You're still wearing that coat.

YOUNG WIFE. Put it with my hat.

He takes off her coat and puts it on the sofa beside the other things.

And now – goodbye.

YOUNG MASTER. Emma! Emma!

YOUNG WIFE. Your five minutes are up.

YOUNG MASTER. You've not even been here a minute!

YOUNG WIFE. I want to know the exact time, Alfred.

YOUNG MASTER. It's exactly … six fifteen.

YOUNG WIFE. I should have been at my sister's ages ago.

YOUNG MASTER. You can see your sister anytime you like.

YOUNG WIFE. Oh, Alfred, why did you get me to do this?

YOUNG MASTER. Because … Emma … I adore you.

YOUNG WIFE. How many women have you said that to?

YOUNG MASTER. None, since I met you.

YOUNG WIFE. I must be out of my mind. If someone had said, just a week ago … just yesterday …

YOUNG MASTER. Though we did arrange this the day before yesterday.

YOUNG WIFE. You kept pestering me. It wasn't me that wanted it. God knows, I didn't want to. I made my mind up yesterday … I even wrote you a long letter, you know, last night.

YOUNG MASTER. I didn't get it.

YOUNG WIFE. I tore it up. Oh, I knew I should have sent it!

YOUNG MASTER. It's a good thing you didn't.

YOUNG WIFE. No, it isn't, it's disgraceful … of me … What have I been thinking? Goodbye, Alfred, let me go.

He hugs her and showers her face with kisses.

But you promised. You did.

YOUNG MASTER. One more kiss – one more.

YOUNG WIFE. The very last.

He kisses her. She returns it. A long kiss.

YOUNG MASTER. Shall I tell you something, Emma? I've just found out what happiness is.

She sits back in the armchair. He sits on the arm of the chair and drapes his arm round her.

Or rather: what it *would* be.

She sighs deeply. He kisses her again.

YOUNG WIFE. Oh Alfred, Alfred, what are you doing to me?

YOUNG MASTER. It's not too bad, this place, is it? And we're so safe here. This is miles better than having to meet outdoors somewhere.

YOUNG WIFE. Don't remind me.

YOUNG MASTER. We had our moments. I shall always remember them – every precious minute I've been able to spend with you.

YOUNG WIFE. Remember the Directors' Institute Ball?

YOUNG MASTER. Of course. I sat next to you at dinner, right up close. And that champagne your husband . . .

She looks at him reproachfully.

I was just going to talk about the champagne. Which reminds me – what about a glass of brandy, Emma?

YOUNG WIFE. Just a tiny one. But give me a glass of water first.

YOUNG MASTER. Of course . . . Now, where's the, um, ah yes.

He draws the curtain and goes into the bedroom. She watches him. He returns with a jug of water and two glasses.

YOUNG WIFE. Where did you go?

YOUNG MASTER. To the ... other room.

Pours water.

YOUNG WIFE. I've got to ask you a question, Alfred, and you must promise to tell me the truth.

YOUNG MASTER. I promise.

YOUNG WIFE. Have there ever been any other women here?

YOUNG MASTER. Emma, this house has been here for twenty years.

YOUNG WIFE. You know what I mean, Alfred. Here, with you.

YOUNG MASTER. With me? Here? Oh, Emma, how could you think that?

YOUNG WIFE. So you ... how shall I ... No, I won't ask you. It's better that I don't ask. Anyway, I'm guilty myself. We reap what we sow.

YOUNG MASTER. What are you talking about? What do you mean, reap what we sow?

YOUNG WIFE. No, no, I mustn't think about it ... I'll die of shame if I do.

YOUNG MASTER (*holding the water-jug, shakes his head sadly*). Emma, if you knew how you've hurt me.

She pours herself a brandy.

Let me say something, Emma. If you're ashamed to be here – if I mean so little to you – if you can't see that you are everything to me – then you'd better go.

YOUNG WIFE. Yes, I think I'd better.

YOUNG MASTER (*taking her hand*). But if you can see that I can't live without you; that it means more to me just to be able to kiss your hand than it would to make love to any other woman ... Emma, I'm not like the rest of them, with all their sweet talk. Maybe I'm just naïve ... I ...

YOUNG WIFE. But what if you *are* just like the rest of them?

YOUNG MASTER. If I were, you wouldn't be here – because you're not like other women.

YOUNG WIFE. How can you tell?

YOUNG MASTER (*has taken her to the sofa and is sitting beside her*). I've been thinking about you a lot. I know how unhappy you are.

YOUNG WIFE (*pleased*). Yes.

YOUNG MASTER. Life is so empty, so meaningless – and it's so short, so terribly short. Your only chance of happiness is ... to find someone who loves you.

She takes a candied pear and pops it into her mouth.

Half for me.

She offers it to him between her lips.

YOUNG WIFE (*stops his hands from wandering*). What do you think you're doing, Alfred? Is that how you keep your promise?

YOUNG MASTER (*swallowing the pear, more boldly*). Life is so short.

YOUNG WIFE (*weakly*). But that doesn't mean –

YOUNG MASTER (*mechanically*). Yes, it does.

YOUNG WIFE (*more feebly*). But Alfred, you absolutely promised to behave ... anyway, it's so bright in here.

YOUNG MASTER. You know, don't you, that you're the only one ... my one and only ... my darling ... come on ...

He lifts her up from the sofa.

YOUNG WIFE. What are you doing?

YOUNG MASTER. It's not so bright in there.

YOUNG WIFE. Is that ... another room?

YOUNG MASTER (*takes her with him*). A lovely one ... and it's dark.

YOUNG WIFE. Perhaps we should stay in here.

But he is now on the other side of the curtain and in the bedroom with her, unlacing her bodice.

You're so ... Oh my God, what are you doing to me? ... Alfred!

YOUNG MASTER. I worship you, Emma.

YOUNG WIFE. All right, hold on, just give me a minute ... Go away ... I'll call you, when ...

YOUNG MASTER. Here, let me help that off – you with that off – help you ... off, with, that ...

YOUNG WIFE. Careful. You're tearing everything.

YOUNG MASTER. You're not wearing a corset?

YOUNG WIFE. Certainly not. Darling, no one does nowadays. But you can undo my shoes for me if you like.

He takes her shoes off and kisses her feet. She slips into bed.

Ooh, it's so cold.

YOUNG MASTER. It'll be warm soon enough.

YOUNG WIFE (*laughing*). You think so?

YOUNG MASTER (*irritated, to himself*). Meaning what?

Undresses.

YOUNG WIFE (*tenderly*). Come here. Come here.

YOUNG MASTER (*cheered up*). Coming.

YOUNG WIFE. Lovely smell of violets here.

YOUNG MASTER. You're my violet. Yes . . .

Joining her.

You.

YOUNG WIFE. Alfred! Alfred!

YOUNG MASTER. Emma!

• •

YOUNG MASTER. I'm obviously too much in love with
    you . . . that's why . . . I can't cope with this . . .

YOUNG WIFE. . . .

YOUNG MASTER. You know, these last few days, I've been
    going crazy. I thought this might happen.

YOUNG WIFE. Don't worry about it.

YOUNG MASTER. No, of course not. It's perfectly normal,
    obviously, when . . .

YOUNG WIFE. Don't . . . you're working yourself up. Just
    calm down . . .

YOUNG MASTER. Have you read Stendhal?

YOUNG WIFE. What?

YOUNG MASTER. Stendhal's *On Love*?

YOUNG WIFE. Why d'you ask?

YOUNG MASTER. Well, there's a story in it – which says a lot.

YOUNG WIFE. What sort of story?

YOUNG MASTER. Well, a group of cavalry officers are chatting together.

YOUNG WIFE. And?

YOUNG MASTER. They're talking about their love lives. And each one says that the woman he loved the most ... most passionately, you know ... she made him ... well, with her he ... well, to cut a long story short, it's the same for them as it was with me, just now.

YOUNG WIFE. I see.

YOUNG MASTER. It's very common. But that's not all. One of them says ... that this never happened to him. But Stendhal says he was a terrible bragger.

YOUNG WIFE. Oh.

YOUNG MASTER. But it's irritating. That's the silly thing. Even though it really doesn't matter.

YOUNG WIFE. Of course it doesn't. But actually, you know ... you did promise to be good.

YOUNG MASTER. Don't tease me. It doesn't help, you know.

YOUNG WIFE. I'm not. It's very interesting what Stendhal says. I thought it only happened with much older men ... or with very ... you know, men who'd lived it up.

YOUNG MASTER. What?! It's got nothing to do with that. By the way, I forgot Stendhal's best story. One of these cavalry officers says he once spent three whole nights ... or was it six, I can't remember ... with a woman he'd wanted for weeks – you know, *désirée* – and all they did, the whole night long, was cry for joy ... both of them.

YOUNG WIFE. Both of them?

YOUNG MASTER. Yes. Are you surprised? To me, that's so understandable – precisely because they're in love.

YOUNG WIFE. But there must be lots of people who don't cry.

YOUNG MASTER (*irritable*). Obviously . . . That was just an extreme case.

YOUNG WIFE. I see. I thought Stendhal meant that all cavalry officers cry in that situation.

YOUNG MASTER. Now you're just making fun of me again.

YOUNG WIFE. Not at all. Do grow up, Alfred.

YOUNG MASTER. Well, it gets on my nerves. And I get the impression you're thinking about it the whole time. It's making me embarrassed.

YOUNG WIFE. I'm not thinking about it at all.

YOUNG MASTER. I know. If only I knew that you loved me.

YOUNG WIFE. What else can I do?

YOUNG MASTER. It's just that . . . well, you keep teasing me.

YOUNG WIFE. There now . . . come here, my darling, give me your little head.

YOUNG MASTER. Oh, that feels good.

YOUNG WIFE. Do you love me?

YOUNG MASTER. Oh, I'm so happy.

YOUNG WIFE. But you don't have to cry about that too.

YOUNG MASTER (*pulling back. Very irritated*). There you go again. And I asked you specially.

YOUNG WIFE. What, when I say that you don't have to cry for joy?

YOUNG MASTER. You said: cry about that *too*.

YOUNG WIFE. You're getting all worked up, my love.

YOUNG MASTER. I know.

YOUNG WIFE. But you shouldn't be. I'm glad that . . . that we'll be parting as friends.

YOUNG MASTER. You're doing it again!

YOUNG WIFE. Don't you remember? What we said, the first time we met? Just good friends. That was so nice . . . at my sister's, remember, at New Year's, we were dancing a quadrille . . . Oh God! I should have gone hours ago . . . my sister's expecting me – what am I going to tell her? . . . Goodbye, Alfred.

YOUNG MASTER. Emma! How can you leave me like this?

YOUNG WIFE. Like what?

YOUNG MASTER. Five more minutes.

YOUNG WIFE. All right. Five minutes. But will you promise . . . to keep still? All right? I'll give you one more goodbye kiss . . . shh . . . be quiet . . . don't move, I said, or I'll get up straight away, my sweet . . . sweet . . .

YOUNG MASTER. Emma . . . my darling . . .

• •

YOUNG WIFE. Oh Alfred. –

YOUNG MASTER. Ah . . . God in heaven . . .

YOUNG WIFE. Now I've really got to go.

YOUNG MASTER. Oh, your sister can wait.

YOUNG WIFE. I mean, go home. It's too late to go to my sister's now. In fact, what *is* the time?

YOUNG MASTER. How should I know?

YOUNG WIFE. Maybe by looking at your watch.

YOUNG MASTER. It's in my waistcoat pocket.

YOUNG WIFE. Well, go and get it then.

YOUNG MASTER (*springs to his feet with a mighty bound*). It's eight.

YOUNG WIFE (*sits up quickly*). Oh Christ ... Quick, Alfred, pass me my stockings. What am I going to say? They'll be expecting me back by now ... Eight o'clock ...

YOUNG MASTER. When will I see you again?

YOUNG WIFE. Never.

YOUNG MASTER. Emma! So you don't love me any more.

YOUNG WIFE. Exactly. Pass me my shoes.

YOUNG MASTER. Never see me again? Here you are.

YOUNG WIFE. There's a button-hook in my handbag. Hurry up ...

YOUNG MASTER. Here.

YOUNG WIFE. Alfred – we've had it.

YOUNG MASTER (*aghast*). What do you mean?

YOUNG WIFE. Well, what am I going to say when he asks me where I've been?

YOUNG MASTER. You've been at your sister's.

YOUNG WIFE. Fine, if I was any good at lying.

YOUNG MASTER. Well, you're going to have to learn.

YOUNG WIFE. The things I have to do for you. Come here ... let me kiss you one more time.

She hugs him.

Now – leave me, go into the other room. I can't get dressed with you here.

The YOUNG MASTER *goes into the sitting room and gets dressed. He eats some of the candied fruit and drinks a cognac. Pause.*

Alfred!

YOUNG MASTER. Darling.

YOUNG WIFE. It's perhaps just as well we didn't cry about it.

YOUNG MASTER (*smiling with a trace of pride*). How can you be so flippant?

YOUNG WIFE. What's it going to be like now – if we bump into each other again somewhere?

YOUNG MASTER. Bump into each other? You'll be at the Lobheimers' tomorrow, surely?

YOUNG WIFE. Yes. Will you?

YOUNG MASTER. Of course. Will you reserve the cotillon for me?

YOUNG WIFE. Then I can't possibly go. How do you expect me to . . . ? I'd just . . .

She comes into the sitting room fully dressed and helps herself to a chocolate.

. . . die.

YOUNG MASTER. Well then, tomorrow, at the Lobheimers'. That's settled.

YOUNG WIFE. No, no . . . I'll cancel, obviously I will –

YOUNG MASTER. All right, the day after tomorrow, then . . . here.

YOUNG WIFE. You can't be serious.

YOUNG MASTER. Around six.

YOUNG WIFE. I'll be able to find a cab on the corner, will I?

YOUNG MASTER. As many as you like. Well, then. Six
o'clock, here, day after tomorrow. Say yes, my darling.

YOUNG WIFE. We'll talk about it during the cotillon
tomorrow.

YOUNG MASTER (*embracing her*). My angel.

YOUNG WIFE. Careful. Don't mess my hair up all over again.

YOUNG MASTER. Tomorrow, then, at the Lobheimers'. And
the day after tomorrow, here, in my arms.

YOUNG WIFE. 'Bye.

YOUNG MASTER (*suddenly worried*). And what are you going
to tell him – tonight?

YOUNG WIFE. Don't ask ... just don't ask ... it's just too
awful. – Oh, why must I love you so much? ... Goodbye. I'll
have a fit if I meet anyone on the stairs again. Oh, what the
hell ...

He kisses her hand again. She leaves.

YOUNG MASTER (*left alone. He sits on the sofa and breaks into
a smile*). Well now, here I am, having an affair with a
respectable married woman.

5. The Young Wife and the Husband

A comfortable bedroom. It is half past ten at night. The YOUNG
WIFE *is in bed, reading. The* HUSBAND *enters in his dressing gown.*

YOUNG WIFE (*without looking up*). Work all done?

HUSBAND. I'm too tired. And besides –

YOUNG WIFE. What?

HUSBAND. I suddenly felt so lonely at my desk. I found myself
missing you.

YOUNG WIFE (*looking up*). Really?

HUSBAND (*sits beside her on the bed*). Don't read any more
tonight. It'll ruin your eyes.

YOUNG WIFE (*closes the book*). So what's up?

HUSBAND. Nothing, darling. I love you. You know that.

YOUNG WIFE. One could sometimes almost forget.

HUSBAND. Sometimes one *should* forget.

YOUNG WIFE. Why is that?

HUSBAND. Because otherwise marriage would be incomplete.
It would ... how can I put this ... it would lose its sanctity.

YOUNG WIFE. Really ...

HUSBAND. No, it's true ... If, in the five years we've been
married, we hadn't sometimes forgotten that we were in love
with each other – well, then, we wouldn't still be in love
now.

YOUNG WIFE. You've lost me.

HUSBAND. My point is simply this: you and I have had, what, a dozen love affairs – all with each other. Isn't that how it feels to you?

YOUNG WIFE. I haven't been counting.

HUSBAND. If we'd had the whole meal, as it were, at one sitting; if I'd given in to my passion straight away – well, then we'd be no better off now than millions of other couples. Our relationship would be over.

YOUNG WIFE. Oh, I see what you mean.

HUSBAND. Believe me, Emma, I was worried at first that that might happen.

YOUNG WIFE. Me too.

HUSBAND. Do you see? I was right, wasn't I? And that's why it's good, sometimes, just to live together as good friends.

YOUNG WIFE. I see.

HUSBAND. And that way we've been able to keep on having honeymoons, because I never let them . . .

YOUNG WIFE. Go on for months.

HUSBAND. Exactly.

YOUNG WIFE. And so now – we're about to be more than just good friends again?

HUSBAND (*embracing her*). Indeed.

YOUNG WIFE. But what if – I didn't feel the same way?

HUSBAND. But you do feel the same way. Because you're the cleverest and most delightful person in the world. I'm so happy to have found you.

YOUNG WIFE. How nice. You can be very flattering – now and then.

HUSBAND (*takes off his dressing gown and gets into bed*). For a man who's seen the world a bit – here, rest your head against my shoulder – for a man who's seen the world, marriage is a much more mysterious thing than it is for you young girls from good families. You come to us pure and . . . well, at least to a certain extent . . . ignorant. And because of that, you actually have a much clearer conception of the true meaning of love than we do.

YOUNG WIFE (*laughing*). Oh!

HUSBAND. It's true. We get confused and discouraged by all the different experiences we've had to go through before marriage. Of course, you young women hear a great deal, and know more than you should, and you definitely read too much; but even so, you don't really appreciate what it's like for us men. You see, we end up being put off this thing that everyone calls love, after . . . let's face it, after the kind of creatures we've had to turn to.

YOUNG WIFE. And what kind of creatures are they?

HUSBAND (*kisses her on the forehead*). Just be grateful, my darling, that you've had no glimpse of anything of that kind. Anyway, you have to feel sorry for most of them. Let us not cast the first stone.

YOUNG WIFE. What's all this sympathy? If you ask me, they don't deserve any.

HUSBAND (*indulgently*). Oh, but they do. You girls from good homes, your parents looking after you while you wait quietly for some decent fellow to come along and propose; – you have no idea of the poverty that drives most of these wretches into the arms of sin.

YOUNG WIFE. So they do it just for the money, do they?

HUSBAND. I wouldn't put it like that. I don't just mean

material poverty. There's also such a thing as, how shall I
say, *moral* poverty: a deficient grasp of what's proper ...
above all, of what is noble.

YOUNG WIFE. But why do you feel sorry for them? – They
have a perfectly good life, don't they?

HUSBAND. You have some strange ideas, my darling. You
mustn't forget, they're doomed to sink deeper and deeper.
There's no stopping.

YOUNG WIFE (*snuggling closer to him*). It sounds quite nice, this
sinking.

HUSBAND (*in pained surprise*). How can you talk like that,
Emma? I'd have thought a respectable woman would find
nothing more disgusting than one who isn't.

YOUNG WIFE. Of course, Karl, of course. I was just saying.
Go on. It's so nice when you talk like this. Tell me more.

HUSBAND. What about?

YOUNG WIFE. Well – these creatures.

HUSBAND. What's got into you?

YOUNG WIFE. Oh, go on. I've asked you before, haven't I?
Right from the start, I was always asking to hear about you
as a young man.

HUSBAND. Why are you so interested?

YOUNG WIFE. Well, you're my husband, aren't you? And I
just think it's unfair for me to know so little about your past.

HUSBAND. You surely don't think I'd be so tasteless as to –
no, that's enough, Emma ... Is nothing sacred?

YOUNG WIFE. Even so, you've ... Who knows how many
other young ladies you've held like this?

HUSBAND. They weren't ladies. *You're* a lady.

YOUNG WIFE. But you've got to tell me one thing ... or else ... or else ... no more honeymoon.

HUSBAND. What a way to talk ... remember, you're a mother ... and that's our little girl asleep in there ...

YOUNG WIFE (*cuddling him*). But I want a little baby boy too.

HUSBAND. Emma!

YOUNG WIFE. Oh, come on, don't be such a ... Of course, I'm your wife ... but once in a while I'd like to be ... your lover.

HUSBAND. Would you now? ...

YOUNG WIFE. But – first, my question.

HUSBAND (*indulgently*). Well?

YOUNG WIFE. Were ... any of them ... married women?

HUSBAND. What do you mean?

YOUNG WIFE. You know.

HUSBAND (*uneasily*). What makes you ask?

YOUNG WIFE. I want to know if ... I mean, I know there are women like that ... but whether you ... ?

HUSBAND (*sternly*). Do you know any women like that?

YOUNG WIFE. I've no idea.

HUSBAND. Is one of your friends a woman of that kind, by any chance?

YOUNG WIFE. How could I possibly tell? I mean, for certain?

HUSBAND. Has any of your friends ever ... People talk about all kinds of things – I mean, when it's just women together – has anyone ever owned up ... ?

YOUNG WIFE (*uncertain*). No.

HUSBAND. Do you *suspect* that any of your friends has ... ?

YOUNG WIFE. Suspect? ... Oh ... suspect.

HUSBAND. You obviously do.

YOUNG WIFE. Of course not, Karl. Definitely not. Now that I think about it – none of them would.

HUSBAND. None of them?

YOUNG WIFE. None of my friends.

HUSBAND. Promise me one thing, Emma.

YOUNG WIFE. Well?

HUSBAND. That if you ever have even the slightest reason to think someone is ... leading anything other than a completely respectable life, you'll have nothing to do with her.

YOUNG WIFE. Do I really have to promise that?

HUSBAND. Of course, I know you'd never spend time with a woman like that deliberately. But you might by chance ... in fact, women whose reputations leave something to be desired often seek out the company of decent women. Partly to help their standing, but also from a ... how shall I put it? ... a certain nostalgia for their virtue.

YOUNG WIFE. I see.

HUSBAND. Yes, in fact that's spot-on. A nostalgia for virtue. Because, take my word for it, these women are dreadfully unhappy.

YOUNG WIFE. Why?

HUSBAND. What a question, Emma! – How can you ask? – Just imagine the kind of life these women have to lead. Full of lies, deception, meanness ... and full of danger.

YOUNG WIFE. Yes, you're right.

HUSBAND. Absolutely – they pay for their little bit of happiness ... What am I saying, happiness? ... Their little bit of ...

YOUNG WIFE. Pleasure.

HUSBAND. Pleasure? Why do you call it pleasure?

YOUNG WIFE. Well – it must be something – ! Or they wouldn't do it, would they?

HUSBAND. It's just a ... thrill.

YOUNG WIFE (*thoughtfully*). A thrill.

HUSBAND. Not even that. But whatever it is – it comes at a high price, that's for sure.

YOUNG WIFE. So ... you once partook – did you?

HUSBAND. Yes, Emma ... It's my most painful memory.

YOUNG WIFE. Who? Tell me. Do I know her?

HUSBAND. Emma, what are you talking about?

YOUNG WIFE. Was it a long time ago? Was it very long before you married me?

HUSBAND. Don't ask. Please don't ask.

YOUNG WIFE. But Karl.

HUSBAND. She's dead.

YOUNG WIFE. Seriously?

HUSBAND. Yes ... it sounds ridiculous, but my impression is that these women all die young.

YOUNG WIFE. Did you love her very much?

HUSBAND. One can't love a liar.

YOUNG WIFE. So why . . .

HUSBAND. The thrill . . .

YOUNG WIFE. Is that right?

HUSBAND. Can we not talk about it any more, please. It was all so very long ago. I've only ever loved one woman – and that's you. One can only love where there is purity and truth.

YOUNG WIFE. Karl!

HUSBAND. Oh, how safe, how good one feels in arms like these. Oh, why didn't I know you when you were still a child? I don't think I would ever have looked at another woman.

YOUNG WIFE. Karl!

HUSBAND. And you're beautiful! . . . beautiful . . . Oh . . .

He turns the light out.

. . . .

YOUNG WIFE. Know what tonight reminds me of?

HUSBAND. What, my darling?

YOUNG WIFE. Of . . . of . . . Venice.

HUSBAND. Our first . . . night . . .

YOUNG WIFE. Yes . . . you've . . .

HUSBAND. What? Go on, say it.

YOUNG WIFE. You've been so sweet tonight.

HUSBAND. Of course.

YOUNG WIFE. Oh . . . if only you were always . . .

HUSBAND (*in her arms*). What?

YOUNG WIFE. Karl! My darling!

HUSBAND. What? If only I were always what?

YOUNG WIFE. You know.

HUSBAND. And what if I were always . . . ?

YOUNG WIFE. Then I'd always know that you love me.

HUSBAND. Yes, but surely you know that anyway. A man can't always be the loving husband, you know; sometimes he has to go out into the hostile world, he has to fight the good fight. Never forget that, my darling. There's a time for everything in marriage – that's what's so beautiful about it. Not many couples, you know, five years on, still – remember Venice.

YOUNG WIFE. Absolutely.

HUSBAND. And now . . . goodnight . . . my little darling.

YOUNG WIFE. Goodnight.

6. The Husband and the Sweet Young Thing

A private room in the restaurant 'zum Riedhof'. Subdued comfortable elegance. The gas fire is burning. On the table the remains of a meal – cream pastries, fruit, cheese etc. Hungarian white wine. The HUSBAND *is smoking a Havana cigar, leaning back in one corner of the sofa. The* SWEET YOUNG THING *is sitting in an armchair beside him, spooning down whipped cream from a pastry with evident pleasure.*

HUSBAND. D'you like that?

SWEET YOUNG THING (*without a pause*). Mmmm!

HUSBAND. Fancy another?

SWEET YOUNG THING. I've had too much already.

HUSBAND. You've finished your wine.

He pours her some more.

SWEET YOUNG THING. No more, sir ... please, I'll just leave it.

HUSBAND. So formal again!

SWEET YOUNG THING. Well – you see, sir – it's hard breaking the habit.

HUSBAND. You see?

SWEET YOUNG THING. What?

HUSBAND. You just called me 'sir' again. – Come and sit next to me.

SWEET YOUNG THING. In a mo' – I've not finished this yet.

He gets up, goes behind the chair, and tries to turn her head towards him.

What is it?

HUSBAND. I want you to kiss me.

SWEET YOUNG THING (*gives him a kiss*). You are naughty, aren't you, sir? . . . Oops.

HUSBAND. Have you only just noticed?

SWEET YOUNG THING. No, I thought so earlier . . . even outside, sir.

HUSBAND. There you go again.

SWEET YOUNG THING. You must think I'm – well . . .

HUSBAND. What?

SWEET YOUNG THING. Well, me going into a private room with you like this. Straight away.

HUSBAND. Not really straight away.

SWEET YOUNG THING. But you did ask so nicely.

HUSBAND. Do you think?

SWEET YOUNG THING. And anyway, what does it matter?

HUSBAND. Exactly.

SWEET YOUNG THING. Whether you go out for a walk, or –

HUSBAND. Anyway, it's much too cold to go for a walk.

SWEET YOUNG THING. Exactly. *Much* too cold.

HUSBAND. But it's lovely and warm in here, eh?

He sits back down again, and pulls her with him.

SWEET YOUNG THING (*weakly*). Oh dear.

HUSBAND. Now, tell me ... You spotted me earlier on, didn't you?

SWEET YOUNG THING. Of course. In the Singerstrasse.

HUSBAND. I don't mean today. I mean the day before yesterday, when I followed you. And the day before that.

SWEET YOUNG THING. I get followed quite a lot.

HUSBAND. I bet. But did you notice me?

SWEET YOUNG THING. Well, sir ... sorry ... you know what happened the other day? I got followed all the way home by my cousin's husband. He couldn't tell it was me, it was that dark.

HUSBAND. Did he try to pick you up?

SWEET YOUNG THING. Honestly, you cheeky thing! Not everyone's as naughty as you are, you know.

HUSBAND. But it does happen.

SWEET YOUNG THING. Course it does.

HUSBAND. So what do you do then?

SWEET YOUNG THING. Nothing. – I don't answer.

HUSBAND. Hmm ... But you answered me.

SWEET YOUNG THING. Are you cross about that?

HUSBAND (*kisses her hard*). Your lips taste of whipped cream.

SWEET YOUNG THING. They're sweet enough already.

HUSBAND. Have lots of other men told you that?

SWEET YOUNG THING. Lots!? Who do you think I am?

HUSBAND. Come on, tell me the truth. How many men have kissed you on the mouth?

SWEET YOUNG THING. What sort of a question is that?
And anyway, you wouldn't believe me if I told you.

HUSBAND. And why not?

SWEET YOUNG THING. Well, guess then.

HUSBAND. I'd say – but don't be cross.

SWEET YOUNG THING. Why would I be cross?

HUSBAND. All right then, I'd say ... twenty.

SWEET YOUNG THING (*moving away*). Huh! – why not a
hundred?

HUSBAND. Just guessing.

SWEET YOUNG THING. Well, it's not a very good guess.

HUSBAND. All right, ten then?

SWEET YOUNG THING (*offended*). Well, I suppose if a girl
lets herself get chatted up by a man in the street and goes to
a private room with him straight away ...

HUSBAND. Don't be childish. What does it matter whether
you walk round town together or sit together indoors ...
Anyway, this is a restaurant. The waiter could come in any
minute – it's perfectly respectable.

SWEET YOUNG THING. Just what I was thinking.

HUSBAND. Have you ever been in one of these private rooms
before?

SWEET YOUNG THING. Well, to tell you the truth, I have.

HUSBAND. Good. At least you're honest.

SWEET YOUNG THING. But it wasn't like what you're
thinking. I was with my friend and her fiancé at Carnival
last year.

HUSBAND. It wouldn't be the end of the world, you know, if you'd been with – your boyfriend . . .

SWEET YOUNG THING. Course not. But I haven't got a boyfriend.

HUSBAND. Oh, come on.

SWEET YOUNG THING. I haven't. Honest.

HUSBAND. But you're not trying to tell me that I'm the . . .

SWEET YOUNG THING. What? . . . I've not had a boyfriend for – at least six months.

HUSBAND. I see . . . So who was he, then?

SWEET YOUNG THING. Why do you want to know?

HUSBAND. Because . . . I've fallen for you.

SWEET YOUNG THING. Really?

HUSBAND. Of course. Couldn't you tell? So come on, out with it.

Draws her to him.

SWEET YOUNG THING. What do you want me to say?

HUSBAND. Don't be such a tease, now. I want to know who he was.

SWEET YOUNG THING (*laughing*). Well, he was a man.

HUSBAND. So tell me about him.

SWEET YOUNG THING. He was a bit like you.

HUSBAND. Really.

SWEET YOUNG THING. If you hadn't looked so much like him . . .

HUSBAND. What then?

SWEET YOUNG THING. Do I have to say? I think you know ...

HUSBAND (*understands*). So that's why you didn't mind when I approached you.

SWEET YOUNG THING. I suppose so.

HUSBAND. I don't know whether to be pleased or annoyed.

SWEET YOUNG THING. You should be pleased.

HUSBAND. Maybe.

SWEET YOUNG THING. The way you talk reminds me of him too ... and the way you look at me.

HUSBAND. What was he?

SWEET YOUNG THING. Look at your eyes, I can't believe it!

HUSBAND. What was his name?

SWEET YOUNG THING. Stop it. Stop looking at me like that, can't you?

He embraces her and gives her a long passionate kiss. She shakes herself free and tries to stand up.

HUSBAND. Where are you going?

SWEET YOUNG THING. It's time I went home.

HUSBAND. Later.

SWEET YOUNG THING. No, I really have to go home. What do you think my mother's going to say?

HUSBAND. You live with your mother?

SWEET YOUNG THING. Course. Where did you think I lived?

HUSBAND. I see – with your mother. Just you and her, then, is it?

SWEET YOUNG THING. You must be joking. There's five of us. Two boys and two more girls.

HUSBAND. Don't sit so far away. Are you the oldest?

SWEET YOUNG THING. No, I'm the second. The oldest is Kathi; she works in a flower shop. Then there's me.

HUSBAND. And what do you do?

SWEET YOUNG THING. I stay at home.

HUSBAND. The whole time?

SWEET YOUNG THING. Someone's got to stay at home.

HUSBAND. I see. And what do you tell your mother when you – come home as late as this?

SWEET YOUNG THING. It doesn't happen that often.

HUSBAND. What about tonight? Your mother will ask you, won't she?

SWEET YOUNG THING. Course she will. Doesn't matter how careful I am – she always wakes up when I come in.

HUSBAND. So what will you say?

SWEET YOUNG THING. Well, maybe that I've been to see a show.

HUSBAND. And will she believe you?

SWEET YOUNG THING. Why shouldn't she? I go to the theatre loads of times. Last Sunday we went to the opera, me and my friend and her fiancé and my older brother.

HUSBAND. How did you get the tickets?

SWEET YOUNG THING. My brother's a hairdresser.

HUSBAND. What? . . . Oh, a hairdresser at the theatre, you mean?

SWEET YOUNG THING. Why d'you keep asking me these questions?

HUSBAND. I want to know these things. And what does your other brother do?

SWEET YOUNG THING. He's still at school. He wants to be a teacher. Imagine.

HUSBAND. So you've got a younger sister too?

SWEET YOUNG THING. Yes, she's just a kid, but you've still got to keep an eye on her. You wouldn't believe what these schoolgirls get up to. The other day I caught her going out on a date.

HUSBAND. Really?

SWEET YOUNG THING. Yup. Walking down the Strozzigasse with a boy from the school opposite, she was. At seven-thirty in the evening as well. I ask you.

HUSBAND. And what did you do?

SWEET YOUNG THING. I gave her a belting.

HUSBAND. Are you always so strict?

SWEET YOUNG THING. Someone's got to be. My older sister's out at work, my mum just moans. – So it's down to me.

HUSBAND. Oh God, you're so sweet.

Kisses her and gets more intimate.

You remind me of someone too.

SWEET YOUNG THING. Oh yeah? Who?

HUSBAND. No one especially ... you remind me of when ...
well, of my youth. Anyway, drink up, dear girl.

SWEET YOUNG THING. So how old are you then? Hey ...
I don't even know your name yet.

HUSBAND. I'm Karl.

SWEET YOUNG THING. I don't believe it. Your name's
Karl?

HUSBAND. Was he called Karl too?

SWEET YOUNG THING. No. But still, it's amazing ... that
look.

Shakes her head.

HUSBAND. You still haven't told me anything about him.

SWEET YOUNG THING. He was no good, that's for sure ...
Or else he wouldn't have walked out on me.

HUSBAND. Were you very fond of him?

SWEET YOUNG THING. Course I was fond of him.

HUSBAND. I know: he was a lieutenant.

SWEET YOUNG THING. No, he wasn't in the army. They
wouldn't take him. His father has a house in ... but why am
I telling you all this?

HUSBAND (*kisses her*). Your eyes are actually grey. I thought at
first they were black.

SWEET YOUNG THING. Does that mean they're not pretty
enough for you?

He kisses her eyes.

No, don't, please, I can't bear that ... please, please ... Oh
God ... No, let me stand up ... just for a moment, please.

HUSBAND (*more tenderly*). No, no, no.

SWEET YOUNG THING. Please, Karl, don't.

HUSBAND. So how old are you then? Eighteen?

SWEET YOUNG THING. Just turned nineteen.

HUSBAND. Nineteen? ... And I'm ...

SWEET YOUNG THING. Thirty.

HUSBAND. And the rest. Let's not talk about it.

SWEET YOUNG THING. He was thirty-two when I met him.

HUSBAND. When was that?

SWEET YOUNG THING. I can't remember ... You know, I think there's something in the wine.

HUSBAND. What do you mean?

SWEET YOUNG THING. I'm a bit ... you know – my head's spinning.

HUSBAND. Well, then hold me tight. There ...

He draws her closer to him and caresses her more and more intimately. She hardly resists.

I tell you what, my darling, we could go now if you like.

SWEET YOUNG THING. Yes ... home.

HUSBAND. Well, not straight home ...

SWEET YOUNG THING. What do you mean? ... Oh no, oh no ... I couldn't possibly ... what an idea.

HUSBAND. Listen, my sweet, next time we meet, we'll, you know, sort something out, so that ...

He has sunk to the floor and put his head in her lap.

That's good, oh, that's so good.

SWEET YOUNG THING. What're you doing?

She kisses his hair.

There was definitely something in that wine – I'm so sleepy ... Hey, what if I can't get up? But ... Karl ... what if someone comes in ... please ... the waiter.

HUSBAND. He's not going to be ... coming ... in ...

• •

She is leaning back with her eyes shut in the corner of the sofa. He is walking up and down, smoking a cigar. Long pause.

HUSBAND (*looks at her for while. Then to himself*). God knows what kind of girl she is – Dear God ... it was all so quick ... not very careful of me.

SWEET YOUNG THING (*without opening her eyes*). Must have been something in that wine.

HUSBAND. Why do you say that?

SWEET YOUNG THING. Well, otherwise ...

HUSBAND. Why do you blame it all on the wine?

SWEET YOUNG THING. Where've you gone? Why are you so far away? Come here.

He goes over to her and sits down.

Now tell me if you really like me.

HUSBAND. But you know ...

Breaks off quickly.

Of course I do.

SWEET YOUNG THING. You see ... it's really ... come on, tell me the truth, what was in that wine?

HUSBAND. What do you take me for?

SWEET YOUNG THING. Well, I just don't get it. I'm not usually like this ... we've only known each other for ... I'm not like that ... I swear to God – If you thought I was ...

HUSBAND. Oh come on – what are you getting so upset about? I don't think the worse of you. I just think you like me.

SWEET YOUNG THING. Yes ...

HUSBAND. After all, if two young people in a room together have dinner and drink some wine ... there doesn't have to be anything in the wine.

SWEET YOUNG THING. I was just talking.

HUSBAND. Yes, but why?

SWEET YOUNG THING (*slightly proud*). I was ashamed.

HUSBAND. How ridiculous. There's no reason for that. Especially since I remind you of your first lover.

SWEET YOUNG THING. Yes.

HUSBAND. Your very first.

SWEET YOUNG THING. Well ...

HUSBAND. But now I want to know about the others.

SWEET YOUNG THING. There weren't any.

HUSBAND. That's not true. It can't be.

SWEET YOUNG THING. Please don't go on at me.

HUSBAND. D'you want a cigarette?

SWEET YOUNG THING. No, thank you.

HUSBAND. D'you know what time it is?

SWEET YOUNG THING. No.

HUSBAND. Half past eleven.

SWEET YOUNG THING. Really?

HUSBAND. What about your mother, then? Used to this, is she?

SWEET YOUNG THING. Are you packing me off home already?

HUSBAND. But that's what you wanted earlier.

SWEET YOUNG THING. Gosh, you've changed. What have I done?

HUSBAND. What do you mean, my dear? You're imagining things.

SWEET YOUNG THING. It was ... it was the way you looked at me, I swear ... Otherwise, you'd never have ... Lots of men have begged me to go with them to private rooms before.

HUSBAND. Well, would you like to ... come here again soon, with me ... or somewhere else, perhaps.

SWEET YOUNG THING. I don't know.

HUSBAND. What's that supposed to mean: you don't know?

SWEET YOUNG THING. Well go on then, ask me.

HUSBAND. All right then – when? Oh, by the way, I'd better tell you: I don't actually live in Vienna. I ... just come here now and then. For a few days at a time.

SWEET YOUNG THING. Really – you're not Viennese?

HUSBAND. Of course I'm Viennese. But nowadays I live not far from –

SWEET YOUNG THING. Where?

HUSBAND. What difference does it make, for God's sake?

SWEET YOUNG THING. Well don't worry, I'm not coming after you.

HUSBAND. No, come if you like. Really. I live in Graz.

SWEET YOUNG THING. Do you mean it?

HUSBAND. Of course I do. Why?

SWEET YOUNG THING. You're married, aren't you?

HUSBAND (*very surprised*). What makes you think that?

SWEET YOUNG THING. It just looks that way.

HUSBAND. Say I was, would that bother you?

SWEET YOUNG THING. Well, I'd prefer it if you were single. – But you *are* married, aren't you?

HUSBAND. Oh, come on, why do you say that?

SWEET YOUNG THING. When a man says he doesn't live in town, and that he can't always find the time –

HUSBAND. But that's not impossible, is it?

SWEET YOUNG THING. I don't believe him.

HUSBAND. And you'd have a clear conscience, would you, about leading a married man astray?

SWEET YOUNG THING. Huh! I bet your wife's up to the same thing.

HUSBAND (*outraged*). That's enough. How dare you!

SWEET YOUNG THING. But I thought you didn't have a wife.

HUSBAND. Whether or not I have a wife – I will not have you making remarks like that.

He's stood up.

SWEET YOUNG THING. Oh Karl, what is it, Karl? Are you cross with me? Look, I didn't know you were married. I was just talking. Come on, come here and let's be friends.

HUSBAND (*goes over to her after a few seconds*). You really are strange creatures, you ... females.

He caresses her further.

SWEET YOUNG THING. No ... don't ... and it's getting really late.

HUSBAND. Now, look here. Let's talk seriously for a moment. I want to see you again. I want to see more of you.

SWEET YOUNG THING. Do you mean that?

HUSBAND. But it would mean ... well, I'd have to trust you. I couldn't keep an eye on you.

SWEET YOUNG THING. Oh, I can look after myself.

HUSBAND. You're ... well, not inexperienced, exactly – but young – and most men are unscrupulous.

SWEET YOUNG THING. I'll say.

HUSBAND. I don't just mean morally ... well, you know what I mean.

SWEET YOUNG THING. Look, what do you think I am?

HUSBAND. Well then – if you want me as your lover – me and no one else – well, we can sort something out – even though I do live in Graz. This wasn't quite right, was it –

She snuggles up to him.

Next time ... we'll go somewhere else, all right?

SWEET YOUNG THING. All right.

HUSBAND. Where we'll be completely undisturbed.

SWEET YOUNG THING. Yes.

HUSBAND (*embraces her closely*). We'll talk about the rest on the way home.

Gets up, opens the door.

Waiter . . . the bill.

7. The Sweet Young Thing and the Poet

A small room, tastefully and comfortably furnished. Curtains which leave the room in semi-darkness. Red net curtains. A large writing desk littered with books and papers. An upright piano against the wall. The SWEET YOUNG THING *and the* POET *come in together. He locks the door.*

POET. So, my darling.

Kisses her.

SWEET YOUNG THING (*in hat and cloak*). Ooh, it's nice here. Except you can't see a thing.

POET. Your eyes need to adjust to the half-light – These sweet eyes!

Kisses her eyelids.

SWEET YOUNG THING. These sweet eyes aren't going to have time for that.

POET. Why not?

SWEET YOUNG THING. Because I'm only staying a minute.

POET. Take your hat off, then.

SWEET YOUNG THING. For just one minute?

POET (*takes the pin out and puts the hat to one side*). And your coat.

SWEET YOUNG THING. What are you up to? I'm going to have to leave soon.

POET. But you need a rest first. We've been walking for three hours.

SWEET YOUNG THING. We were in a carriage.

POET. Coming home, yes – but in Weidling we walked for
three whole hours. So sit yourself down, my darling . . .
wherever you like . . . here, at my desk . . . but no, that's not
comfortable. Sit on the divan.

Sits her down.

There we are. If you're very tired, you can have a lie-down.
Like this.

He lays her down.

With your little head on the cushion.

SWEET YOUNG THING (*laughing*). But I'm not a bit tired.

POET. That's what you think. There you are – and if you're
sleepy, you can have a snooze. I'll be as quiet as a mouse. I
can even play you a lullaby – one of my lullabies.

Goes to the piano.

SWEET YOUNG THING. One of yours?

POET. Yes.

SWEET YOUNG THING. But I thought you were a professor,
Robert.

POET. Really? But I've told you I'm a writer.

SWEET YOUNG THING. But writers are all professors,
aren't they?

POET. Not all. Not me, for example. But why did you bring
that up?

SWEET YOUNG THING. Because you said you wrote that
tune you're playing.

POET. Ah . . . maybe it's not one of mine after all. It doesn't
really matter, does it? Who cares who wrote it, as long as it's
beautiful – don't you think?

SWEET YOUNG THING. Absolutely ... as long as it's
    beautiful – that's the main thing! –

POET. Do you know what I meant by that?

SWEET YOUNG THING. What?

POET. What I just said.

SWEET YOUNG THING (*sleepily*). Of course.

POET (*goes over to her and strokes her hair*). You didn't understand
    a word, did you?

SWEET YOUNG THING. Huh, I'm not that stupid.

POET. Of course you're that stupid. But that's just what I love
    about you. It's wonderful when women are stupid. I mean
    the way you are.

SWEET YOUNG THING. I don't know why you're being so
    horrid.

POET. My little angel. Cosy there on that nice soft rug, are
    you?

SWEET YOUNG THING. Yes. Go on then, play something
    else.

POET. I'd rather sit here with you.

Strokes her.

SWEET YOUNG THING. Can't you light a lamp or
    something?

POET. Oh, no ... The twilight feels so good. We spent the
    whole day as if bathing in sunbeams. Now we have emerged
    from the bath, as it were, and wrapped ourselves ... in the
    twilight, like a bathrobe.

Laughs.

Oh no – that doesn't sound right ... what do you think?

SWEET YOUNG THING. Dunno.

POET (*moving away*). Such divine stupidity.

He takes out a notebook and starts to write.

SWEET YOUNG THING. What are you doing?

Turns round to look at him.

What's that you're writing?

POET (*under his breath*). Sun, bath, twilight – cloak ... That's it.

He puts the notebook in his pocket and laughs.

Nothing ... And now, my little treasure, would you like something to eat or drink?

SWEET YOUNG THING. Actually, I'm not a bit thirsty. But I am hungry.

POET. Hm ... I'd rather you were thirsty. I've got brandy, but I'd have to go out for food.

SWEET YOUNG THING. Can't someone do that for you?

POET. That's tricky. The maid's not here right now – hang on – I'll go myself ... what would you like?

SWEET YOUNG THING. It's really not worth the bother. I must get home, anyway.

POET. Sweet, I won't hear of it. Tell you what, though: on our way out we can stop off for supper somewhere.

SWEET YOUNG THING. Oh no, I don't have time for that. And besides, where would we go? Someone might recognise us.

POET. Do that many people know you?

SWEET YOUNG THING. It only takes one to see us, and the damage is done.

POET. What sort of damage?

SWEET YOUNG THING. Well, just think if my mum found out . . .

POET. We could go where no one will see us; some restaurants have private rooms.

SWEET YOUNG THING (*singing*). 'Oh, in a private room, just you and me . . . '

POET. Have you ever been in a private room?

SWEET YOUNG THING. To tell you the truth, I have.

POET. Who was the lucky man?

SWEET YOUNG THING. Oh, it wasn't like that . . . It was with my girlfriend and her fiancé. They took me.

POET. Really. And you expect me to believe that?

SWEET YOUNG THING. You don't have to believe me.

POET (*close to her*). Are you blushing? It's getting so dark. I can scarcely make out your face.

Feels her cheek with his hand.

But I can feel it.

SWEET YOUNG THING. Well, mind you don't mix me up with someone else.

POET. It's extraordinary, I really can't remember what you look like.

SWEET YOUNG THING. Thanks a lot!

POET (*seriously*). You know, this is weird, I just can't picture you. – In a certain sense, I've forgotten you already – now, if I couldn't remember the sound of your voice either . . . what actually would you be? – So near; and, yet, so far . . . weird.

SWEET YOUNG THING. What are you on about?

POET. Nothing, my angel, absolutely nothing. Now, where are your lips ... ?

Kisses her.

SWEET YOUNG THING. Why don't you light the lamp?

POET. Oh, no ...

Becoming very affectionate.

Tell me, do you love me?

SWEET YOUNG THING. Very much ... very much.

POET. Have you ever loved anybody as much?

SWEET YOUNG THING. Like I said, no.

POET. But ...

Sighs.

SWEET YOUNG THING. Well, there was my fiancé.

POET. I'd rather you didn't think about him right now.

SWEET YOUNG THING. Oi ... what are you up to ... hang on ...

POET. We could pretend we're in a palace in India.

SWEET YOUNG THING. I bet they wouldn't be as bad there as you are.

POET. How idiotic! It's divine – If only you knew what you mean to me ...

SWEET YOUNG THING. Well?

POET. Stop pushing me away; I've not done anything – so far.

SWEET YOUNG THING. Hey, my corset hurts.

POET (*simply*). So take it off.

SWEET YOUNG THING. All right, but don't get ideas.

POET. No.

She gets up and takes off her corset in the dark. He sits down on the sofa.

Don't you want to know my surname, though?

SWEET YOUNG THING. Yes, so what's your name?

POET. Rather than tell you my name, I'll tell you what I'm called.

SWEET YOUNG THING. What's the difference?

POET. Well, what I'm called as a writer.

SWEET YOUNG THING. So you don't write under your real name?

He moves very close to her.

Hey! ... please ... don't.

POET. What a sweet smell.

He kisses her breasts.

SWEET YOUNG THING. You're ripping my blouse.

POET. Off with it. Off with these ... superfluities.

SWEET YOUNG THING. But Robert!

POET. And now come inside our Indian palace.

SWEET YOUNG THING. Tell me first if you really love me.

POET. But I worship you!

He has pushed her down onto the divan. Kisses her fervently.

I worship you, my treasure, my springtime ... my ...

SWEET YOUNG THING. Robert ... Robert ...

• •

POET. Ye gods, that was out of this world . . . I'm called . . .

SWEET YOUNG THING. Robert, oh my Robert.

POET. I'm called Biebitz.

SWEET YOUNG THING. Why are you called Biebitz?

POET. It's not my name, it's what I'm called . . . don't you
know that name?

SWEET YOUNG THING. No.

POET. You don't know the name Biebitz? How divine. Really?
You're just saying that, aren't you?

SWEET YOUNG THING. Cross my heart. Never heard it.

POET. Don't you go to the theatre, then?

SWEET YOUNG THING. Oh yes – Just the other day I went
with a – with my girlfriend's uncle and my girlfriend. We
went to the Opera, to see *Cavalleria*.

POET. Hmm. So you've never been to the Burgtheater?

SWEET YOUNG THING. I don't get free tickets for there.

POET. I'll send you a ticket next time.

SWEET YOUNG THING. Oh, yes. But don't forget. For
something funny, though.

POET. Yes . . . funny . . . So you don't want to go to something
sad?

SWEET YOUNG THING. Not really.

POET. Even if it's by me?

SWEET YOUNG THING. What? – by you? You write plays,
then?

POET. May I . . . I'm just going to light a candle. I've not
looked at you since we became lovers. – My angel.

Lights a candle.

SWEET YOUNG THING. Don't. I'm embarrassed. Give me a blanket at least.

POET. In a minute.

Goes to her with the candle and looks at her face for a long while.

SWEET YOUNG THING (*covers her face with her hands*). Robert. Don't.

POET. You're beautiful ... you're Beauty, maybe even Nature itself ... you are what is simple and holy.

SWEET YOUNG THING. Ouch, careful with that wax. Watch what you're doing.

POET (*puts the candle down*). You're what I've been looking for. You love me for what I am, and you'd love me even if I was a draper's assistant. That makes me glad. I must admit I wasn't quite sure until now. Tell me the truth: did you never suspect that I was Biebitz?

SWEET YOUNG THING. Look, I don't know what you want me to say. I don't know anyone called Biebitz.

POET. Such is fame. No, forget everything I said, forget even the name I told you. I am, and for you I will always be Robert. I was only joking.

Lightly.

I'm not a writer, I'm a shop assistant and in the evening I play the piano in a band.

SWEET YOUNG THING. Well, now I'm completely confused ... and the way you look at a girl. What's the matter with you? What is it?

POET. This is so strange – it's hardly ever happened to me before, my darling, but I'm close to tears. You touch me so deeply. We want to be together, don't we? We'll be so in love.

SWEET YOUNG THING. Is that true, then, about you playing in a band?

POET. Yes, but don't ask any more. If you love me, ask nothing at all. Tell me, could you get away for a couple of weeks?

SWEET YOUNG THING. What do you mean, get away?

POET. Well, away from home.

SWEET YOUNG THING. What?! How could I do that? What would my mum say? And they'd get in a right mess at home.

POET. I thought it would be so beautiful, just the two of us together for a week or two, somewhere alone, in the woods. I can see us now, communing with nature, living the natural life. Just us ... in the wild. And then one day, goodbye! – to part forever, to go we know not where.

SWEET YOUNG THING. What's all this goodbye stuff? I thought you liked me.

POET. That's why –

Bends over and kisses her on the forehead.

You sweet creature.

SWEET YOUNG THING. Hold me tight, I'm so cold.

POET. It's time you got dressed. Wait, I'll light some more candles for you.

SWEET YOUNG THING (*gets up*). Don't look.

POET. No.

At the window.

Tell me, my darling, are you happy?

SWEET YOUNG THING. What do you mean?

POET. I mean in general. Are you happy?

SWEET YOUNG THING. Things could be better.

POET. You misunderstand me. You've told me enough about your domestic arrangements. I know you're not a princess. But I mean, when you put all that to one side, when you just feel alive. Do you ever actually feel alive?

SWEET YOUNG THING. Hey, don't you have a comb?

POET (*goes to the dressing table, gives her the comb and watches her*). My God, you're enchanting.

SWEET YOUNG THING. Don't.

POET. Look, stay a bit ... stay ... I'll go and get something for dinner, and ...

SWEET YOUNG THING. But it's much too late.

POET. It's not even nine yet.

SWEET YOUNG THING. I know, but I've got to get going.

POET. When are we going to see each other again?

SWEET YOUNG THING. Well, when do you want to see me again?

POET. Tomorrow?

SWEET YOUNG THING. What day is tomorrow?

POET. Saturday.

SWEET YOUNG THING. I can't do that, I have to take my little sister to see her godfather.

POET. Sunday then ... hmm ... Sunday ... on Sunday ... I should explain. – You see, I'm not Biebitz, but Biebitz is a friend of mine. I'll introduce you to him one day. Anyway,

Biebitz's play is on on Sunday. I'll send you a ticket and pick you up from the theatre afterwards. You can tell me how you liked the play, all right?

SWEET YOUNG THING. All this Biebitz stuff ... I just don't get it.

POET. I'll only really know you, when I know what you think about the play.

SWEET YOUNG THING. There ... I'm ready.

POET. Come along then, my darling girl.

They leave.

8. The Poet and the Actress

A room in a country inn. It is a spring evening, the hills and the fields are bathed in moonlight, and the windows are open. A great stillness. The POET *and the* ACTRESS *enter; the oil-lamp that he is carrying goes out.*

POET. Damn ...

ACTRESS. What is it?

POET. The lamp. – But we won't need it. Look how bright the night is. Amazing.

She suddenly sinks to her knees at the window, with her hands folded.

What is it?

She is silent. He goes over to her.

What are you doing?

ACTRESS (*exasperated*). Can't you see I'm praying?

POET. Do you believe in God?

ACTRESS. Of course, what do you think I am?

POET. I see.

ACTRESS. Come here and kneel beside me. You can pray too, for once. It won't kill you.

He kneels beside her and grabs her.

You dirty –

Silence. She stands up.

D'you know who I was praying to?

POET. God, I assume.

ACTRESS (*scornfully*). Absolutely. I was praying to you.

POET. So why were you staring out the window?

ACTRESS. Where have you dragged me off to, you seducer?

POET. It was your idea, darling. You insisted on going to the country – here, in fact.

ACTRESS. Well, wasn't I right?

POET. Definitely. It's quite magical. Just two hours from Vienna – and total seclusion. What a place.

ACTRESS. Isn't it? You could write a bit of poetry here – if you happened to have any talent.

POET. Have you ever been here before?

ACTRESS. Have I what? I lived here for years.

POET. Who with?

ACTRESS. Fritz, of course.

POET. I see.

ACTRESS. I worshipped that man.

POET. So you've already said.

ACTRESS. Oh, pardon me – I'll leave at once if I'm boring you.

POET. You, bore me? ... You've no idea what you mean to me ... You're the world to me ... You're a goddess, genius itself ... You're ... divine simplicity ... yes, you. But stop talking about Fritz, please.

ACTRESS. All right, that *was* out of character. There.

POET. I'm glad you can see that.

ACTRESS. Come and kiss me.

He kisses her.

And now it's time to say goodnight. Farewell, my treasure.

POET. What do you mean?

ACTRESS. I'm going to bed.

POET. Fine – but what's all this goodnight business? ... I mean, where am I going to sleep?

ACTRESS. I'm sure they have lots of other rooms here.

POET. I'm not interested in the other rooms. Incidentally, we could do with some light in here, don't you think?

ACTRESS. Yes.

POET (*lights the lamp on the bedside table*). What a charming room ... and the people here are so devout. These simple pictures of saints ... It would be interesting to spend some time here, wouldn't it ... It's another world. We know so little about other people, don't we?

ACTRESS. Stop talking nonsense and pass me my bag, will you? It's on the table.

POET. Here you are, my one and only.

She takes a small framed picture out of the bag and puts it on the bedside table.

What's that?

ACTRESS. The Madonna.

POET. Do you always carry her around with you?

ACTRESS. She brings me luck. Now off you go, Robert.

POET. I don't think that's very funny. Don't you want me to give you a hand?

ACTRESS. No. I want you to clear off.

POET. And when shall I come back?

ACTRESS. In about ten minutes.

POET kisses her.

POET. See you soon.

ACTRESS. Where are you going?

POET. I'm going to walk up and down outside your window. I love walking about in the night. I get my best ideas that way. And especially when I'm near you, breathing your sighs of longing ... enmeshed in your art.

ACTRESS. You're talking like an idiot.

POET *(sadly)*. Some women might have said ... like a poet.

ACTRESS. Can you just go. And don't start anything with the barmaid.

He leaves. She undresses and listens to him going downstairs, then pacing around beneath the window. As soon as she is undressed, she goes to the window, looks down, sees him standing there and calls out in a whisper.

Come on!

He comes back up in a hurry and rushes over to her. In the meantime she has gone to bed and put out the light. He locks the door.

Right, now you can sit next to me and tell me something.

POET *(sitting down beside her)*. Shouldn't I close the window? Aren't you cold?

ACTRESS. Not really.

POET. What do you want me to tell you?

ACTRESS. So, who are you being unfaithful to? Right now.

POET. Sorry to say, nobody. Right now.

ACTRESS. Well, don't worry, I'm betraying someone too.

POET. I can imagine.

ACTRESS. And who do you think it is?

POET. Now how would I know?

ACTRESS. Oh go on, guess.

POET. Let me see ... Well, your director.

ACTRESS. Darling boy, I'm not a chorus girl.

POET. It was just an idea.

ACTRESS. Have another guess.

POET. Let me think. Your co-star ... Benno.

ACTRESS. Ha! He doesn't like women at all ... didn't you
   know? He's having an affair with the postman.

POET. You're joking! –

ACTRESS. Anyway, give me a kiss.

   He hugs her.

   What are you doing?

POET. Don't torture me like this.

ACTRESS. Listen, Robert, let me make a suggestion. Lie down
   here beside me.

POET. It's a deal.

   He undresses quickly.

ACTRESS. Come on, come on.

POET. Actually ... if I'd had my way, I'd have done that long
   ago ... Listen ...

ACTRESS. What?

POET. The crickets chirping.

ACTRESS. Don't be silly, darling, you don't get crickets round here.

POET. But you can hear them.

ACTRESS. Come on!

POET. Here I am.

Joins her.

ACTRESS. And now just lie there quietly ... ssh ... don't move.

POET. What's the idea?

ACTRESS. You'd really like to have an affair with me, wouldn't you?

POET. That should be obvious to you by now.

ACTRESS. So would many others ...

POET. But you can't deny that, right now, I'm in the lead.

ACTRESS. Come on then, my cricket. I'm going to call you cricket from now on.

POET. How nice ...

• •

ACTRESS. So, who am I betraying?

POET. I really couldn't care less ...

• •

ACTRESS. That was more fun than acting in stupid plays ... don't you think?

POET. I think it's good that sometimes you get to act in a decent play.

ACTRESS. You arrogant dog, I bet you mean yours again.

POET. I certainly do!

ACTRESS (*seriously*). It really is a masterly play.

POET. You see.

ACTRESS. Yes, you're a great genius, Robert.

POET. This might be the occasion for you to tell me why you cancelled the other night. There was absolutely nothing wrong with you.

ACTRESS. Well, I wanted to annoy you.

POET. Why? What have I done?

ACTRESS. You were arrogant.

POET. How?

ACTRESS. Everyone at the theatre thinks so.

POET. I see.

ACTRESS. But I told them: that man's entitled to be arrogant.

POET. And what did they say?

ACTRESS. What can they say? I don't talk to anyone.

POET. Oh, I see.

ACTRESS. What they'd all love to do is poison me. But they won't succeed.

POET. Don't think about other people. Just be glad we're here and tell me you love me.

ACTRESS. Do you need further proof?

POET. You can never prove that.

ACTRESS. That's a bit rich. What more do you want?

POET. How many others have you tried to prove it to like this . . . did you love them all?

ACTRESS. Oh no. I've only ever loved one.

POET (*embracing her*). My . . .

ACTRESS. Fritz.

POET. My name's Robert. What am I to you, if now you're thinking about Fritz?

ACTRESS. A passing fancy.

POET. I'm glad I know.

ACTRESS. But tell me, aren't you proud?

POET. Proud of what?

ACTRESS. I think you have every reason to be.

POET. Oh, that.

ACTRESS. Yes, that, my pale cricket! – So, how's the chirping going? Are they still chirping?

POET. Non-stop. Can't you hear it?

ACTRESS. Of course I can hear it. But those are frogs, my darling.

POET. No, you're wrong. Frogs croak.

ACTRESS. Absolutely, they croak.

POET. But not here, my darling. That's chirping.

ACTRESS. You're the most stubborn fellow I've ever met. Give me a kiss, my little frog.

POET. Please don't call me that. It gets on my nerves.

ACTRESS. Well, what should I call you?

POET. I've got a name. Robert.

ACTRESS. Oh, this is too stupid.

POET. All the same, I'd just like you to call me by my name.

ACTRESS. All right then, Robert, give me a kiss ... ah!

Kisses him.

Satisfied, froggie?

Laughs.

POET. Mind if I smoke a cigarette?

ACTRESS. I'll have one too.

He takes out two cigarettes, lights them both, and gives her one.

By the way, you've not said a word about my triumph last night.

POET. What triumph?

ACTRESS. Oh, come on.

POET. Ah, that. I wasn't there.

ACTRESS. You must be joking.

POET. Certainly not. Since you'd cancelled the night before last, I presumed you wouldn't be at your best yesterday, so I stayed away.

ACTRESS. You really missed something.

POET. Did I.

ACTRESS. It was sensational. People went pale.

POET. You could actually see that, could you?

ACTRESS. Benno said: 'Darling, you acted like a goddess.'

POET. Hm ... and you so sick the day before.

ACTRESS. Yes, I was. And do you know why? I was pining for you.

POET. You said earlier that you cancelled just to annoy me.

ACTRESS. But what do you know about my love for you? It leaves you completely cold. And there I was, running a fever the whole night long. A hundred and five degrees!

POET. That's pretty high for a passing fancy.

ACTRESS. You call it a passing fancy? I'm dying of love for you and you call it a passing fancy – ?

POET. And Fritz?

ACTRESS. Fritz? . . . Don't talk to me about that pathetic wretch!

9. The Actress and the Count

The ACTRESS's *bedroom. Opulently furnished. It is midday, the blinds are still down, a candle is burning, and the* ACTRESS *is still in her four-poster bed. The bedspread is covered with newspapers. The* COUNT *enters, wearing the uniform of a captain of the dragoons. He stands at the door.*

ACTRESS. Ah, Count . . .

COUNT. Your dear Mama said it was all right, otherwise I'd never have –

ACTRESS. Oh, do come in, please.

COUNT. Dear lady. Must apologise – coming straight in from the street like this . . . can't see a thing yet. Ah yes . . . here we are.

Near the bed.

At your service.

ACTRESS. Do sit down, dear Count.

COUNT. Your Mama said you weren't well. Nothing serious, one hopes.

ACTRESS. Serious? I was dying.

COUNT. Good Lord.

ACTRESS. Anyway, it's sweet of you to be . . . so concerned.

COUNT. Dying? And last night you acted like a goddess.

ACTRESS. I know.

COUNT. Astonishing. The audience was knocked out. To say nothing of myself.

ACTRESS. Thank you for the lovely flowers.

COUNT. Not at all.

ACTRESS (*indicating with her eyes a large basket of flowers on a little table*). They're over there.

COUNT. You were showered with bouquets.

ACTRESS. I left them all in my dressing room. Yours were the only ones I brought home.

COUNT (*kisses her hand*). You're very kind.

She suddenly takes his and kisses it.

I say.

ACTRESS. Don't be alarmed, Count. This doesn't commit you to anything.

COUNT. What an extraordinary creature. Mysterious, one might even say.

Pause.

ACTRESS. I suppose Miss Birken is . . . easier to solve?

COUNT. No great mystery there. Not, of course, that one knows her at all well.

ACTRESS. Really?

COUNT. I assure you. But you are a challenge. Always longed for a bit of a challenge. And to think what pleasure I've been denying myself, never to have seen you perform – until last night . . .

ACTRESS. How so?

COUNT. A bit tricky for me, the theatre, you see. Tend to dine late . . . so by the time one's got to the theatre, one's missed the best of it, what?

ACTRESS. Well, from now on you'll have to eat a little earlier.

COUNT. Precisely. Or not at all. Not much pleasure in it, anyway. Dinner.

ACTRESS. What does a young fogey like you know about pleasure?

COUNT. I ask myself the same question. Not a fogey, though. Must be another reason.

ACTRESS. Really?

COUNT. Yes. Old Lulu, now, he says I'm a philosopher. By which he means, you see, that I think too much.

ACTRESS. Yes. Thinking makes one unhappy.

COUNT. Too much time on my hands, you see. That's the thing. Be better, I thought, when I got posted back to Vienna. Plenty here to keep a chap occupied, I thought. Bright lights and all that. But you know, when it comes down to it, it's no different here than there.

ACTRESS. Where's there?

COUNT. Hungary, dear lady. Out in the sticks, mostly. Garrison towns of one sort or another.

ACTRESS. What were you up to in Hungary?

COUNT. Well, as I say, doing one's bit.

ACTRESS. But why were you there so long?

COUNT. Well, these things happen.

ACTRESS. It would drive me mad.

COUNT. Oh, I don't know. One keeps busy. Always something to keep you occupied out there: you know, recruits to be trained, new mounts to be broken in ... and the countryside isn't as bad as people say. Those plains – quite extraordinary. And the sunsets ... make you wish you could paint. Would have painted one of those sunsets myself. Would like to have done that. One chap we had in the regiment, Splany I think his name was, now, he was good at painting. But why am I boring you with all this stuff?

ACTRESS. Please, Count, I'm fascinated.

COUNT. You know, a chap can talk to you. Lulu told me that. Not something you come across very often.

ACTRESS. Well, not in Hungary, I'm sure.

COUNT. Or in Vienna. People are the same everywhere. Where there's more of them, there's more of a crowd. That's the only difference. D'you much care for people yourself?

ACTRESS. I loathe them. Can't bear them. And I don't see anyone. I can be alone here. People don't come bothering me here.

COUNT. As I thought: you're a misanthrope. Must be common in the art world ... all those higher things to deal with ... anyway, you're lucky. At least you know what life's for.

ACTRESS. What makes you think that? I've no idea what life is for.

COUNT. Come now – you're famous – celebrated.

ACTRESS. But is that happiness?

COUNT. Happiness? My dear lady, there's no such thing. In fact, as a rule, the more people go on about something, the more it tends not to exist. Take love, for example. Same thing there.

ACTRESS. You're absolutely right.

COUNT. Pleasure ... intoxication ... now, that's quite different. Those are definite things. I feel pleasure; fine.

I know I'm having pleasure, because I can feel it. Same thing when you're drunk. That's another definite thing. And when it's over, it's over.

ACTRESS (*grandly*). It's over.

COUNT. But as soon as a chap, how shall I put it, as soon as he stops living for the moment – as soon as he starts thinking about afterwards, or before ... well, then he's done for. 'After' ... is sad, and who knows about 'before' ... bang, chap gets all in a muddle. Don't you think?

ACTRESS (*with brimming eyes*). You've cracked it.

COUNT. And once that's clear, d'you see, it doesn't really matter whether a chap's in Vienna, or out on the *puszta*, or in Steinamanger. Let me give you an example ... now, where can I put my cap? ... Ah, most kind ... now, where were we?

ACTRESS. In Steinamanger.

COUNT. So we were. Well, as I say, it comes to much the same thing. Whether I spend the evening in the mess or at the club. It's all one, really.

ACTRESS. And how does all this relate to love?

COUNT. Well, if a chap believes in love, there's always someone.

ACTRESS. Little Miss Birken, for example.

COUNT. I really don't know why you keep coming back to that particular young lady.

ACTRESS. Because she's your mistress.

COUNT. Who says so?

ACTRESS. Everyone knows.

COUNT. Except me. How extraordinary.

ACTRESS. But you fought a duel over her.

COUNT. And got myself shot dead, I suppose, and just didn't notice.

ACTRESS. Well, Count, you are a man of honour. So come a little closer.

COUNT. If I may.

ACTRESS. Over here.

She draws him to her and ruffles his hair with her hand.

I knew you'd call today.

COUNT. How?

ACTRESS. I knew in the theatre yesterday.

COUNT. Could you see me from the stage?

ACTRESS. My dear fellow. Didn't you realise that I was playing for you alone?

COUNT. Surely not.

ACTRESS. When I saw you in the front row, I started trembling all over.

COUNT. Trembling? Because of me? Had no idea you noticed me there.

ACTRESS. Oh, stop being such an awful toff. It's driving me nuts.

COUNT. As you wish, dear lady.

ACTRESS. 'As you wish, dear lady'! ... At least take off that sabre.

COUNT. If I may.

Unbuckles his belt and leans the sabre against the bed.

ACTRESS. And now kiss me. Finally.

He kisses her, she doesn't let him go.

I wish I'd never set eyes on you.

COUNT. But it's better like this.

ACTRESS. Count, you're such a fraud.

COUNT. Me? Why?

ACTRESS. Just think how happy most men would be in your position!

COUNT. But I am.

ACTRESS. I thought you said there was no such thing as happiness. Why are you looking at me like that? You know what, Count, I think you're frightened of me.

COUNT. As I said, dear lady, you're a challenge.

ACTRESS. Please ... no more philosophy ... Come here. And ask me for something ... anything you like. You're too handsome, you dog.

COUNT. Well, then ...

Kisses her hand.

Permission to return this evening.

ACTRESS. This evening? ... But I'm working this evening.

COUNT. After the play.

ACTRESS. Nothing else you'd like?

COUNT. I'll ask for everything else after the play.

ACTRESS (*hurt*). You can ask then till you're blue in the face, you miserable fraud.

COUNT. Look ... we've been frank with each other, all right ... I mean, it would really be so much nicer in the evening, after the play ... jollier than it would be now, with ... well, with that door liable to fly open at any minute, for one thing.

ACTRESS. It doesn't open from the outside.

COUNT. Shame to rush at something and spoil it, I always think. Something potentially very fine.

ACTRESS. 'Potentially'!

COUNT. To be absolutely frank with you, I find love-making in the morning pretty ghastly.

ACTRESS. You are quite the oddest man I've ever met.

COUNT. Now, with your average totty, of course, that doesn't apply. In fact, on the whole, it really makes no odds. But a woman like you – call me old-fashioned, if you like – a woman like you shouldn't be taken before breakfast. There it is, really.

ACTRESS. You're so sweet.

COUNT. You do see what I'm saying, don't you? What I had in mind –

ACTRESS. Go on, tell me.

COUNT. Well, what I had in mind was that . . . after the curtain comes down, I'd wait for you in my carriage; then we'd drive off together for a spot of supper somewhere –

ACTRESS. I'm not Miss Birken.

COUNT. Not suggesting you are. I just find – everything comes down to being in the right mood. Never really properly in the mood, myself, till I've had a bit of supper. And then, you see, one has that lovely drive home together, and then . . .

ACTRESS. What?

COUNT. Well, then it's a question of how matters develop.

ACTRESS. Come closer. Come on.

COUNT (*sits down on bed*). I must say, the perfume on these
pillows – mignonette, is it?

ACTRESS. It's so hot in here, don't you think?

She raises herself slightly under the cover.

He bends down and kisses her throat.

Oh, Count, that isn't on your schedule.

COUNT. Who says? I have no schedule.

She draws him closer.

It is rather hot.

ACTRESS. Isn't it?

COUNT. And so dark, it could almost be evening ...

ACTRESS (*pulling him down towards her*). It *is* evening ... it's
night ... shut your eyes if it's too light. Come here ... come
on ...

He gives in.

• •

ACTRESS. So what was all that about being in the mood, you
fraud?

COUNT. You little devil.

ACTRESS. What *do* you mean?

COUNT. Well, angel, then.

ACTRESS. And you should have been an actor. I mean it. You
really understand women. And do you know what I'm going
to do now?

COUNT. No.

ACTRESS. I'm going to tell you I never want to see you again.

COUNT. Why?

ACTRESS. No, no, you're much too dangerous. You'd drive a woman mad. You stand there as if nothing happened.

COUNT. But ...

ACTRESS. May I remind you, sir, that I've just become your mistress.

COUNT. I shan't forget.

ACTRESS. So what about tonight?

COUNT. What about tonight?

ACTRESS. You were going to meet me at the theatre.

COUNT. Of course. Shall we say the day after tomorrow, then?

ACTRESS. The day after tomorrow? We were talking about tonight.

COUNT. That wouldn't have any real ... meaning.

ACTRESS. You fogey!

COUNT. You misunderstand me. I meant more, how shall I put it, in terms of one's soul.

ACTRESS. What use to me is your soul?

COUNT. It's all part of the same thing, believe me. I think it's a mistake to separate the two.

ACTRESS. No philosophy, please. When I want philosophy, I read a book.

COUNT. But we don't learn anything from books.

ACTRESS. How true. And that's why I want you here tonight. We'll get together for the good of your rotten, stinking soul.

COUNT. May I, then, wait for you in my carriage?

ACTRESS. You'll wait for me here, in my apartment.

COUNT. ... After the play?

ACTRESS. Of course.

He buckles on his sabre.

What are you doing?

COUNT. I think it's time I went. I've stayed rather long for a formal visit.

ACTRESS. Well, it had better not be a formal visit tonight.

COUNT. No?

ACTRESS. Just leave it to me. And now give me another kiss, my little philosopher. There, you seducer ... you sweet man, you soul-destroyer, you rotten stinker ...

Kisses him fervently a few times and then pushes him violently away.

Count, it's been an honour.

COUNT. My compliments, dear lady.

At the door.

Good day to you.

ACTRESS. Au revoir ... Steinamanger.

10. The Count and the Prostitute

It's about six in the morning. A mean little room, with one window. The dirty yellow blinds are down, frayed green curtains. A chest of drawers, with a few photographs on them and a cheap lady's hat in very bad taste. Several cheap Japanese fans behind the mirror. On the table, covered with a reddish cloth, is a kerosene lamp, burning feebly, with a yellow paper lampshade. Next to the lamp is a jug with a little leftover beer, and a half-empty glass. On the floor beside the bed is a disordered pile of women's clothing, apparently discarded in a hurry. The PROSTITUTE *is asleep in bed, breathing evenly. The* COUNT *is on the sofa, fully dressed and in a light overcoat. His hat is on the floor by the sofa.*

COUNT (*moves, rubs his eyes, rises with a start, sits up and looks around*). How did I ... ? So ... So did I really go home with the girl ...

He gets up quickly and sees the bed.

Here she is. How can this happen to a man my age? So how'd I get here? No idea. Did they carry me up here? No, I saw this room, when I came in ... yes, I was still awake then or had woken up, or ... or maybe it's just because the room reminds me of something? ... Dear God, but of course, yes, I saw it last night, that's all.

He looks at his watch.

Last night ... a couple of hours ago? But I knew something was going to happen ... I knew it when I started drinking ... So what did happen? Nothing ... Or did it? ... Dear God ... it's been ten years since this sort of thing last happened to me, as far as I know – ... I must have been so drunk. If only I knew how it started. I do remember going into that

whores' café with Lulu ... no, no ... we left the Hotel
Sacher ... and then on the way it started ... That's right,
Lulu and I were in my carriage ... Why am I racking my
brains about this? It doesn't matter. Let's just get out of
here.

He rises. The lamp rocks.

Oh.

He looks at the sleeping girl.

She's fast asleep. I can't remember a thing, but I'll leave her
some money and ... toodle-oo.

He stands and looks at her for a long time.

If one didn't know what she really was –

Looks at her again.

I've known lots of girls look less virtuous, even in their sleep.
But dear God ... Lulu would say I'm philosophising again,
but it's true, sleep is a great leveller. Like his older brother,
Death ... Hm, I just wish I knew whether I ... No, I'm sure
I'd remember that ... No, no, I collapsed on the sofa
straight away ... and nothing happened ... It's incredible
sometimes how all women can look alike ... Right. Let's go.

He goes to the door.

Oh yes.

Takes out his wallet and is looking for some money.

PROSTITUTE (*waking up*). Um ... Who is it, this early?

Recognising him.

Hello, hon'.

COUNT. Good morning. Sleep well?

PROSTITUTE. Come here. Give us a cuddle.

COUNT. (*bends down, thinks better of it, pulls up short*). I was just on my way out.

PROSTITUTE. You're off?

COUNT. I really have to.

PROSTITUTE. Just like that?

COUNT (*almost embarrassed*). Well . . .

PROSTITUTE. Cheers then. Come back soon.

COUNT. See you. Won't you give me your hand, then?

She pulls her hand out from under the blanket and offers it. He takes her hand, mechanically goes to kiss it, catches himself and laughs.

Like a princess. If all you could see . . .

PROSTITUTE. What you looking at me like that for?

COUNT. . . . was this pretty little head, looking like this . . . they look so innocent when they've just woken up . . . Dear God, you could imagine all kinds of things. If the place didn't stink of paraffin.

PROSTITUTE. That lamp keeps leaking.

COUNT. How old are you, then?

PROSTITUTE. What do you think?

COUNT. Twenty-four.

PROSTITUTE. Thanks.

COUNT. Older?

PROSTITUTE. I ain't twenty yet.

COUNT. And how long have you been . . .

PROSTITUTE. On the game? A year.

COUNT. You started early.

PROSTITUTE. Better early than too late.

COUNT (*sits down on the bed*). Tell me, are you happy?

PROSTITUTE. Eh?

COUNT. I mean, how are things? Are you all right?

PROSTITUTE. Yeah, I'm fine.

COUNT. Good ... Look, have you ever thought of doing something different? With your life?

PROSTITUTE. Like what?

COUNT. Well, you're a beautiful girl. You could take a lover.

PROSTITUTE. You think I don't already?

COUNT. I know – but I mean just one, someone who, you know, could look after you, so you didn't have to go off with just anyone.

PROSTITUTE. I don't have to go off with just anyone. I can pick and choose, thank God.

He looks around the room. She notices.

We're moving into town next month. The Spiegelgasse.

COUNT. We?

PROSTITUTE. Well, me and Madame and a couple of the other girls here.

COUNT. There are others?

PROSTITUTE. Next door ... listen. That's Milli, she was at the café too.

COUNT. That's her snoring?

PROSTITUTE. Yep, that's our Milli. Sleeps all day, gets up at ten at night and goes down to the café.

COUNT. What a terrible life.

PROSTITUTE. It is. And Madame gets fed up with her. Me, I'm always on the street by lunchtime.

COUNT. What do you do on the street at lunchtime?

PROSTITUTE. What do you think? Business ...

COUNT. I see ... yes, of course ...

He gets up, again takes out his wallet and puts money on her bedside table.

Goodbye, then.

PROSTITUTE. Off already? ... Cheers then. Come back soon.

She turns over onto her side.

COUNT (*stops again*). Tell me something. Is it all the same to you nowadays?

PROSTITUTE. Eh?

COUNT. I mean, you never enjoy it any more?

PROSTITUTE (*yawns*). I'm sleepy.

COUNT. All the same to you, whether a chap's young or old, or if he's –

PROSTITUTE. What are you asking?

COUNT. Well ...

Suddenly struck.

My God, now I know who you remind me of.

PROSTITUTE. Who do I look like?

COUNT. It's incredible. Absolutely incredible – please, just don't say anything, please, just for a minute ...

He stares at her.

Exactly the same face, exactly the same . . .

He suddenly kisses her on the eyes.

PROSTITUTE. Huh.

COUNT. God, what a pity you're . . . that you're not . . . You could have made a fortune.

PROSTITUTE. You're just like Franz.

COUNT. Who's Franz?

PROSTITUTE. The waiter at our café.

COUNT. How am I like Franz?

PROSTITUTE. He's always saying I could make a fortune. And that I should marry him.

COUNT. Why don't you?

PROSTITUTE. No thank you very much . . . I don't want to get married. Not a chance. Not yet, anyway.

COUNT. It's your eyes. You have just the same eyes . . . Lulu would say I'm an idiot – but just let me kiss your eyes again. Goodbye now. I'm off.

PROSTITUTE. See ya.

COUNT (*turning at the door*). Listen . . . tell me . . . aren't you surprised?

PROSTITUTE. At what?

COUNT. That I don't want anything from you.

PROSTITUTE. A lot of blokes don't fancy it in the morning.

COUNT. Ah . . .

To himself.

How stupid of me, wanting her to be surprised ...

Well, goodbye then.

At the door.

Actually, it's bothering me. Though, of course, I know that for a girl of her sort it's just about the money. What am I talking about, 'her sort'? Good for her: at least she doesn't pretend. Isn't that so much better? ...

Look, I'm going to come and see you again, all right?

PROSTITUTE (*her eyes closed*). Lovely.

COUNT. When are you usually here?

PROSTITUTE. I'm always here. Just ask for Leocadia.

COUNT. Leocadia ... ? That's pretty. – 'Bye then.

At the door.

I still feel a bit drunk. Extraordinary, isn't it? ... I've just spent the night with a ... and all I did was kiss her eyes because she reminded me of someone else ...

Turns to her.

I say, Leocadia, does this happen often, a chap leaving you like this?

PROSTITUTE. Like what?

COUNT. Like me.

PROSTITUTE. In the morning?

COUNT. No ... I mean have you ever had anyone – who didn't want you to do anything?

PROSTITUTE. Nope.

COUNT. So what do you think? You think it's because I don't like you?

PROSTITUTE. Why would I think that? You liked me last night all right!

COUNT. I like you now, too.

PROSTITUTE. Yeah, but last night you liked me better.

COUNT. Why do you say that?

PROSTITUTE. Oh, come on . . .

COUNT. Last night . . . er . . . you mean, I didn't just collapse on the sofa straight away?

PROSTITUTE. Yeah, you did. With me.

COUNT. With you?

PROSTITUTE. What, don't you remember?

COUNT. I . . . we . . . Right.

PROSTITUTE. And then, straight after – bang, you was out like a light.

COUNT. Straight after. I see . . . It was like that.

PROSTITUTE. Yes, hon'. You must have been really pissed if you can't remember.

COUNT. Indeed . . . still, there is a faint resemblance . . . Goodbye, then.

He listens.

What's that?

PROSTITUTE. The maid's just started. Can you give her something, on your way out?

COUNT. Yes.